PUBLISHED FOR THE USA IN 2024 BY WELBECK CHILDREN'S BOOKS
An imprint of Hachette Children's Group
Part of Hodder & Stoughton Limited
Carmelite House, 50 Victoria Embankment, London, EC4Y 0DZ
An Hachette UK Company
www.hachette.co.uk
www.hachettechildrens.co.uk

All statistical data and player heat maps provided by Opta, under license from Stats Perform.

STATS PERFORM

A catalogue record is available for this book from the British Library.

10 9 8 7 6 5 4 3 2 1
ISBN 978 1 80453 718 3

Printed and bound in Dubai
Author: David Ballheimer
Senior Commissioning Editor: Suhel Ahmed
Design Manager: Matt Drew
Picture research: Paul Langan
Production: Melanie Robertson

PICTURE CREDITS
The publishers would like to thank the following sources for their kind permission to reproduce the pictures in this book.

GETTY IMAGES: AC Milan 51; Ion Alcoba/Quality Sport Images 56; Filippo Alfero/Juventus FC 102; Eric Alonso 27; Emilio Andreoli 20, 103; ANP 28; Franco Arland 61; Gonzalo Arroyo Moreno 48, 76; Marc Atkins 29; Robbie Jay Barratt/AMA 98; Lars Baron 57; James Baylis/AMA 108B; Giuseppe Bellini 17, 97; Berengui/DeFodi Images 8; John Berry 21, 89; Bagu Blanco/Pressinphoto/Icon Sport 10; Shaun Botterill 44; Stefan Brauer/DeFodi Images 106T; Megan Briggs 75; Clive Brunskill 12; David S. Bustamante/Soccrates 22, 66, 80; Pedro Castillo/Real Madrid 34; Jean Catuffe 16; Matteo Ciambelli/NurPhoto 68; Emmanuele Ciancaglini/Ciancaphoto Studio 70; Tim Clayton/Corbis 40; Gareth Copley 106B; Oscar Del Pozo/AFP 111T; Paul Ellis/AFP 85; Gualter Fatia 63; Baptiste Fernandez/Icon Sport 94; Johnny Fidelin/Icon Sport 43; Julian Finney 38; Stuart Franklin 91; Edith Geuppert/GES Sportfoto 39; James Gill/Danehouse 83; Alex Gottschalk/DeFodi Images 33, 60; Stefano Guidi 101; Lionel Hahn 108T; Matthias Hangst 54; Alexander Hassenstein 95; Mike Hewitt 59, 110B; Elie Hokayem/Saudi Pro League 19; Mario Hommes/DeFodi Images 50, 79; Image Photo Agency 108B; Catherine Ivill 11; Fareed Kotb/Anadolu 49; Roland Krivec/DeFodi Images 30; Maurizio Lagana 110T; Christian Liewig/Corbis 100; Alex Livesey 64, 69, 90; Marco Luzzani 65, 73; Stuart MacFarlane/Arsenal FC 53, 107T; Giuseppe Maffia/NurPhoto 55; Manchester City FC 109T; Angel Martinez 24, 26, 62; Clive Mason 105; Matt McNulty/Manchester City FC 35; Mattia Ozbot/Inter 23; Minas Panagiotakis 36; Alex Pantling 41; Andrew Powell/Liverpool FC 7, 25; Pressinphoto/Icon Sport 46; David Price/Arsenal FC 52; Joe Prior/Visionhaus 15; ProShots 111B; Quality Sport Images 88; Manuel Queimadelos/Quality Sport Images 45; Michael Regan 78, 86, 107B; Pedro Salado/Quality Sport Images 14; Fran Santiago 72, 87; Oli Scarff/AFP 5; Silas Schueller/DeFodi Images 71; Juan Manuel Serrano Arce 13; Justin Setterfield 93; Alexandre Simoes/Borussia Dortmund 18, 37; Diego Souto/Quality Sport Images 96; Boris Streubel 74, 92; VI Images 82; Pedro Vilela 77; Visionhaus 9, 31, 42, 47, 67, 81; George Wood 99

Every effort has been made to acknowledge correctly and contact the source and/or copyright holder of each picture; any unintentional errors or omissions will be corrected in future editions of this book.

All facts and stats correct as of June 2024

MEN'S 2025

SOCCER LEGENDS

STATS • PROFILES • TOP PLAYERS

WELBECK
CHILDREN'S BOOKS

CONTENTS

HOW TO USE THIS BOOK

Welcome to *Men's Soccer Legends 2025*—the exciting book packed with the performance stats of the biggest stars in the world of soccer today! We have chosen more than 100 players and managers who have been superstars in the world's top five leagues: The Bundesliga in Germany, La Liga in Spain, France's Ligue 1, the Italian Serie A, and the English Premier League. The players are either playing in or have spent much of their careers up until the 2023/24 season operating in these top leagues.

You can use this book to work out who you think are the best performers comparing the statistical data of today's finest defenders, midfielders, forwards, goalkeepers, and managers.

The types of stats featured for each position vary, because each position performs a specific role on the field. For example, a defender's main job is to stop the opposition from scoring, so the stats focus mainly on this part of that player's game. Likewise, a striker's tackling is not as relevant as the player's goal or assists totals. What you will find for all the players is the heat map, which shows how much of the field a player covers and which areas he focuses his play in or, with goalkeepers, whether their strengths lie in the six-yard box or playing as sweeper keepers who are comfortable all around the penalty area.

The stats span a player's career to date, for the most part playing for teams belonging to one of the top five European leagues. The figures have been collected from only domestic league and European match appearances and exclude data from domestic cups, super cups, or international games. This narrow data pool means that the information is instantly comparable, so you can decide for yourself who truly deserves to be known as a living legend of the beautiful game.

DEFENDERS

There are different types of defenders. They cover a range of positions and have different skills. The centerbacks are the big defenders in the middle who mark the opposition strikers. Fullbacks operate out wide: They are quick, agile, and try to stop wide attackers from crossing balls into the box. Wingers play out wide, too, in front of the centerbacks, but also make attacking runs when they have the chance. Finally, the sweeper is the spare defender who is positioned behind the centerback, ready to help the back four deal with any danger.

WHAT DO THESE STATS MEAN?

75%

AERIAL DUELS WON
This is the percentage of headers a defender has won in his own penalty area to interrupt an opposition attack.

INTERCEPTIONS
This is the number of times a defender has successfully stopped an attack without needing to make a tackle.

BLOCKS
A shot that is intercepted by a defender—preventing his keeper from having to make a save—counts as a block.

KEY PASSES/PASS COMPLETION
A key pass is one that results in an attacking opportunity. Pass completion indicates as a percentage the player's passing accuracy.

CLEARANCES
An attack successfully foiled, either by kicking or heading the ball away from danger, is regarded as a clearance.

TACKLES
This is the number of times a defender has challenged and dispossessed the opposition without committing a foul.

Did you know?

For about 40 years from the late nineteenth century, the most common formation was 2–3–5. It featured only two defenders (right back and left back), while the centerback played in midfield. There were five forwards.

NATIONALITY
Austrian

CURRENT CLUB
Real Madrid

DAVID ALABA

Although his best position is left back, David Alaba's strength is his versatility. Superb with his positioning and reading of the game, his pace and athleticism also allow for him to snuff out attacks before they have begun.

DATE OF BIRTH	06/24/1992
POSITION	LEFT BACK
HEIGHT	5 FT. 10¾ IN.
PRO DEBUT	2007
PREFERRED FOOT	LEFT

BLOCKS
137

APPEARANCES
482

INTERCEPTIONS
598

AERIAL DUELS WON
49%

PASS COMPLETION
89%

PENALTIES SCORED
3

GOALS
33

PASSES
28,753

CLEARANCES
675

TACKLES
586

MAJOR CLUB HONORS

⚽ La Liga: 2022, runner-up 2023, 2024 ⚽ Bundesliga: 2010, 2013–2021 (all B. Munich.) ⚽ UEFA Champions League.: 2013, 2020 (all B. Munich), 2022, 2024 ⚽ FIFA Club World Cup: 2013, 2020 (all B. Munich), 2022 ⚽ UEFA Super Cup: 2022 ⚽ Copa del Rey: 2023

INTERNATIONAL HONORS

⚽ None to date

ACTIVITY AREAS

TRENT ALEXANDER-ARNOLD

Counted among the world's best overlapping defenders, Trent Alexander-Arnold plays at right back or right winger. He is fast, tackles superbly, and is capable of whipping in accurate crosses that strikers love to feast on!

NATIONALITY
English

CURRENT CLUB
Liverpool

66

DATE OF BIRTH	10/07/1998
POSITION	FULLBACK
HEIGHT	5 FT. 9 IN.
PRO DEBUT	2016
PREFERRED FOOT	RIGHT

BLOCKS
36

APPEARANCES
283

INTERCEPTIONS
355

AERIAL DUELS WON
39%

PENALTIES SCORED
0

PASS COMPLETION
78%

GOALS
17

PASSES
17,187

CLEARANCES
405

TACKLES
462

MAJOR CLUB HONORS
⚽ Premier League: 2020 ⚽ UEFA Champions League: 2019
⚽ UEFA Champions League: Runner-up 2018, runner-up 2022
⚽ FIFA Club World Cup: 2019 ⚽ FA Cup 2022

INTERNATIONAL HONORS
⚽ UEFA Nations League: Third place 2019
⚽ UEFA European Championship: runner-up 2024

ACTIVITY AREAS

9

3

NATIONALITY
Spanish

CURRENT CLUB
Atlético Madrid

CÉSAR AZPILICUETA

Right back César Azpilicueta is a natural leader who can play anywhere on the field. He is excellent at using his positional sense to snuff out danger and frequently starts counterattacks with a great right foot.

DATE OF BIRTH	08/28/1989
POSITION	FULLBACK
HEIGHT	5 FT. 10 IN.
PRO DEBUT	2006
PREFERRED FOOT	RIGHT

APPEARANCES
618

BLOCKS
211

INTERCEPTIONS
1,098

AERIAL DUELS WON
57%

PENALTIES SCORED
0

PASS COMPLETION
82%

GOALS
15

PASSES
30,339

CLEARANCES
1,873

TACKLES
1,571

MAJOR CLUB HONORS
⚽ Premier League: 2015, 2017 (Chelsea) ⚽ UEFA Champions League: 2021 (Chelsea) ⚽ UEFA Europa League: 2013, 2019 (all Chelsea) ⚽ FIFA Club World Cup: 2021, runner-up 2012 (Chelsea) ⚽ UEFA Super Cup: 2021 (Chelsea)

INTERNATIONAL HONORS
⚽ UEFA Nations League: Runner-up 2021
⚽ FIFA Confederations Cup: Runner-up 2013

ACTIVITY AREAS

RÚBEN DIAS

Rúben Dias plays mainly on the left side of center defense but is comfortable anywhere along the back line. He excels at winning challenges in the air and on the ground, making interceptions and delivering great passes with both feet.

NATIONALITY
Portuguese

CURRENT CLUB
Manchester City

DATE OF BIRTH	05/14/1997
POSITION	CENTER
HEIGHT	6 FT. 2 IN.
PRO DEBUT	2015
PREFERRED FOOT	RIGHT

BLOCKS
143

APPEARANCES
269

INTERCEPTIONS
257

PENALTIES SCORED
0

AERIAL DUELS WON
58%

PASS COMPLETION
91%

GOALS
15

PASSES
19,572

CLEARANCES
739

TACKLES
323

MAJOR CLUB HONORS
⚽ Premier League: 2021, 2022, 2023, 2024
⚽ UEFA Champions League: Runner-up 2021, 2023
⚽ Portuguese Premier Liga: 2019 (Benfica)
⚽ FA Cup: 2023

INTERNATIONAL HONORS
⚽ UEFA Nations League: 2019

ACTIVITY AREAS

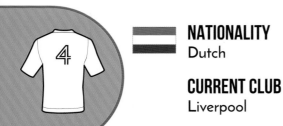

NATIONALITY
Dutch

CURRENT CLUB
Liverpool

VIRGIL VAN DIJK

Virgil van Dijk has returned to the form he showed before his 2020 knee injury. Good with either foot, he is a great tackler, a superb leader, wins headers in both penalty boxes, and reads the game excellently.

DATE OF BIRTH	07/08/1991
POSITION	CENTER
HEIGHT	6 FT. 4¾ IN.
PRO DEBUT	2011
PREFERRED FOOT	RIGHT

BLOCKS
209

APPEARANCES
394*

INTERCEPTIONS
592

AERIAL DUELS WON
75%

PENALTIES SCORED
0

PASS COMPLETION
88%

GOALS
33

PASSES
25,603

CLEARANCES
2,151

TACKLES
445

*Excludes data from Scottish Premiership

MAJOR CLUB HONORS

⚽ Premier League: 2020 ⚽ Scottish Premiership: 2014, 2015 (Celtic) ⚽ UEFA Champions League: 2019, runner-up 2018, runner-up 2022 ⚽ FIFA Club World Cup: 2019 ⚽ FA Cup: 2022

INTERNATIONAL HONORS

⚽ UEFA Nations League: Runner-up 2019

ACTIVITY AREAS

JEREMIE FRIMPONG

Jeremie Frimpong is as comfortable in midfield as he is a winger and fits perfectly in both roles. He uses his great pace and passing ability in attacking situations but has the technical skills to be a great defender.

NATIONALITY
Dutch

CURRENT CLUB
Bayer Leverkusen

30

DATE OF BIRTH	12/10/2000
POSITION	RIGHT WINGER
HEIGHT	5 FT. 7½ IN.
PRO DEBUT	2019
PREFERRED FOOT	RIGHT

BLOCKS
13

APPEARANCES
138*

INTERCEPTIONS
61

AERIAL DUELS WON
39%

PASS COMPLETION
82%

PENALTIES SCORED
0

GOALS
22

PASSES
4,023

CLEARANCES
116

TACKLES
159

*Excludes data from Scottish Premiership

MAJOR CLUB HONORS
⚽ Bundesliga: 2024 ⚽ UEFA Europa League: Runner-up 2024 ⚽ Scottish Premiership: 2020 (Celtic) ⚽ Scottish Cup: 2020

INTERNATIONAL HONORS
⚽ None to date

ACTIVITY AREAS

2

NATIONALITY
Uruguayan

CURRENT CLUB
Atlético Madrid

JOSÉ GIMÉNEZ

The Uruguayan is a tough-tackling centerback who is quick off the mark and difficult to knock off the ball. He made his international debut when he was just 19 and has also thrived at club level since joining Atlético Madrid in 2013.

DATE OF BIRTH	01/20/1995
POSITION	CENTER
HEIGHT	6 FT. ¾ IN.
PRO DEBUT	2012
PREFERRED FOOT	RIGHT

BLOCKS
172

APPEARANCES
287

INTERCEPTIONS
438

AERIAL DUELS WON
65%

PASS COMPLETION
84%

PENALTIES SCORED
0

GOALS
9

PASSES
10,670

CLEARANCES
1,286

TACKLES
409

MAJOR CLUB HONORS
- ⚽ La Liga: 2014, 2021
- ⚽ UEFA Europa League: 2018
- ⚽ UEFA Super Cup: 2018
- ⚽ UEFA Champions League: Runner-up 2014, 2016

INTERNATIONAL HONORS
- ⚽ FIFA U-20 World Cup: Runner-up 2013
- ⚽ China Cup: 2018, 2019

ACTIVITY AREAS

JOŠKO GVARDIOL

The 22-year-old Joško Gvardiol has emerged as one of Europe's most talented defenders. His ability to defend in one-on-one situations, make key interceptions, and tackles are matched by his skills when he turns defense into attack.

NATIONALITY
Croatian

CURRENT CLUB
Manchester City

24

DATE OF BIRTH	10/23/2002
POSITION	CENTER
HEIGHT	6 FT. ¾ IN.
PRO DEBUT	2019
PREFERRED FOOT	LEFT

APPEARANCES
121

INTERCEPTIONS
161

BLOCKS
51

AERIAL DUELS WON
57%

PASS COMPLETION
87%

PENALTIES SCORED
0

GOALS
11

PASSES
8,127

CLEARANCES
224

TACKLES
172

MAJOR CLUB HONORS
⚽ Premier League: 2024
⚽ DFB Pokal: 2022, 2023 (RP Leipzig)
⚽ UEFA Super Cup: 2023
⚽ FIFA Club World Cup: 2023

INTERNATIONAL HONORS
⚽ FIFA World Cup: Third place 2022

ACTIVITY AREAS

2

NATIONALITY
Moroccan

CURRENT CLUB
Paris Saint-Germain

ACHRAF HAKIMI

Born in Spain to Moroccan parents, Ashraf Hakimi has played and enjoyed success at some of Europe's top clubs. Known for his blistering pace and sharp attacking instincts, he can play as a midfielder or winger, and can even score and create goals.

DATE OF BIRTH	11/04/1998
POSITION	RIGHT BACK
HEIGHT	5 FT. 11¼ IN.
PRO DEBUT	2016
PREFERRED FOOT	RIGHT

APPEARANCES
232

BLOCKS
24

INTERCEPTIONS
191

AERIAL DUELS WON
42%

PASS COMPLETION
87%

PENALTIES SCORED
0

GOALS
34

PASSES
12,380

TACKLES
410

CLEARANCES
194

MAJOR CLUB HONORS
⚽ Ligue 1: 2022, 2023, 2024 ⚽ Serie A: 2021 (Inter Milan) ⚽ UEFA Champions League: 2018 (R. Madrid) ⚽ FIFA World Club Cup: 2017 (R. Madrid) ⚽ Coupe de France: 2024

INTERNATIONAL HONORS
⚽ None to date

ACTIVITY AREAS

THEO HERNÁNDEZ

Known more for his attacking qualities than his defensive work, Theo Hernández (younger brother of Lucas) is a soccer player that is blessed with great pace, can dribble rapidly with the ball at his feet, and possesses the capability to get into goal-scoring positions. He has become a fan favorite at AC Milan.

NATIONALITY
French

CURRENT CLUB
AC Milan

19

DATE OF BIRTH	10/06/1997
POSITION	LEFT BACK
HEIGHT	6 FT. ¼ IN.
PRO DEBUT	2015
PREFERRED FOOT	LEFT

APPEARANCES
269

BLOCKS
60

INTERCEPTIONS
264

AERIAL DUELS WON
64%

PASS COMPLETION
84%

PENALTIES SCORED
4

GOALS
30

PASSES
11,794

CLEARANCES
354

TACKLES
426

MAJOR CLUB HONORS
⚽ Serie A: 2022 ⚽ UEFA Champions League: 2018 (R. Madrid) ⚽ FIFA World Club Cup: 2017 (R. Madrid) ⚽ UEFA Super Cup 2017 (R. Madrid)

INTERNATIONAL HONORS
⚽ FIFA World Cup: Runner-up 2022
⚽ UEFA Nations League: 2021

ACTIVITY AREAS

NATIONALITY
German

CURRENT CLUB
TBC

MATS HUMMELS

The German is regarded as one of the best ball-playing defenders on the planet. Hummels can physically tussle with the strongest of forwards, but it is his ability to stride forward and set up attacks with his fine passing that sets him apart.

DATE OF BIRTH	12/16/1988
POSITION	CENTER
HEIGHT	6 FT. 3 IN.
PRO DEBUT	2006
PREFERRED FOOT	RIGHT

BLOCKS
249

APPEARANCES
550

INTERCEPTIONS
1,172

PENALTIES SCORED
1

AERIAL DUELS WON
67%

PASS COMPLETION
85%

GOALS
40

PASSES
33,974

CLEARANCES
2,237

TACKLES
1,292

MAJOR CLUB HONORS

⚽ Bundesliga: 2011*, 2012* (B. Dortmund*), 2017, 2018 (all B. Munich), 2019 (B. Munich), runner-up 2023 (B. Dortmund) ⚽ DFB-Pokal: 2012 (B. Dortmund), 2019 (B. Munich), 2021 (B. Dortmund) ⚽ UEFA Champions League: runner-up 2013, runner-up 2024 (all B. Dortmund)

INTERNATIONAL HONORS

⚽ FIFA World Cup: 2014

ACTIVITY AREAS

AYMERIC LAPORTE

Aymeric Laporte was among Europe's best defenders before moving to the Saudi Pro League in 2023. Very strong, he is a powerful tackler, excellent in the air, and a good organizer at the back. Laporte can also start attacks with his precise passing out of defense.

NATIONALITY
Spanish

CURRENT CLUB
Al Nassr

27

DATE OF BIRTH	05/27/1994
POSITION	CENTER
HEIGHT	6 FT. 2¼ IN.
PRO DEBUT	2011
PREFERRED FOOT	LEFT

BLOCKS
147

APPEARANCES
372

INTERCEPTIONS
656

PENALTIES SCORED
0

AERIAL DUELS WON
65%

PASS COMPLETION
88%

GOALS
21

PASSES
24,208

CLEARANCES
1,278

TACKLES
582

MAJOR CLUB HONORS
⚽ Premier League: 2018, 2019, 2021, 2022, 2023 (all Man. City) ⚽ UEFA Champions League: Runner-up 2021, 2023 (all Man. City) ⚽ FA Cup: 2019, 2023 (all Man. City)

INTERNATIONAL HONORS
⚽ UEFA Nations League: Runner-up 2021, 2023
⚽ UEFA European U-19 Championship: Runner-up 2013 (France)
⚽ UEFA European Championship: 2024

ACTIVITY AREAS

22

NATIONALITY
Italian

CURRENT CLUB
Napoli

GIOVANNI DI LORENZO

Although he began his professional career as an attacking player, Giovanni di Lorenzo is now an excellent defender, normally at right back, but he can play in the middle, too. He has a solid tackling technique, is physically strong, and possesses good aerial ability.

DATE OF BIRTH	08/04/1993
POSITION	RIGHT BACK
HEIGHT	6 FT. 1½ IN.
PRO DEBUT	2010
PREFERRED FOOT	BOTH

APPEARANCES 254

BLOCKS 79

INTERCEPTIONS 222

AERIAL DUELS WON 53%

PASS COMPLETION 86%

PENALTIES SCORED 0

GOALS 19

PASSES 14,618

CLEARANCES 356

TACKLES 461

MAJOR CLUB HONORS
- ⚽ Serie A: 2023
- ⚽ Coppa Italia: 2020

INTERNATIONAL HONORS
- ⚽ UEFA European Championship: 2020 (2021)
- ⚽ UEFA Nations League: Third place 2021, 2023

ACTIVITY AREAS

MARQUINHOS

Marquinhos is a clever defender. He may not be a powerhouse like many of today's top-class centerbacks, but he has the speed, agility, and intelligence to mark the quickest forwards, plus he can be effective going forward.

NATIONALITY
Brazilian

CURRENT CLUB
Paris Saint-Germain

5

DATE OF BIRTH	05/14/1994
POSITION	CENTER
HEIGHT	6 FT.
PRO DEBUT	2012
PREFERRED FOOT	RIGHT

APPEARANCES
407

BLOCKS
258

INTERCEPTIONS
531

AERIAL DUELS WON
58%

PENALTIES SCORED
0

GOALS
33

PASS COMPLETION
93%

PASSES
25,935

TACKLES
610

CLEARANCES
1,382

MAJOR CLUB HONORS
⚽ Ligue 1: 2014, 2015, 2016, 2018, 2019, 2020, 2022, 2023, 2024 ⚽ UEFA Champions League: Runner-up 2020 ⚽ Coupe de France: 2015, 2016, 2017, 2018, runner-up 2019, 2020, 2021, 2024

INTERNATIONAL HONORS
⚽ Copa América: 2019, runner-up 2021
⚽ Olympic Games: 2016

ACTIVITY AREAS

16

NATIONALITY
Argentinian

CURRENT CLUB
Atlético Madrid

NAHUEL MOLINA

Nahuel Molina has worked hard to become a dominant force on the right flank. Very quick, with fine positional sense and good tackling technique, he is also comfortable with the ball at his feet and a tremendous passer in attacking situations.

DATE OF BIRTH	04/06/1998
POSITION	RIGHT BACK
HEIGHT	5 FT. 9 IN.
PRO DEBUT	2016
PREFERRED FOOT	RIGHT

BLOCKS
20

APPEARANCES
143

INTERCEPTIONS
78

AERIAL DUELS WON
38%

PASS COMPLETION
77%

PENALTIES SCORED
0

GOALS
15

PASSES
5,067

CLEARANCES
166

TACKLES
205

MAJOR CLUB HONORS
⚽ None to date

INTERNATIONAL HONORS
⚽ FIFA World Cup: 2022
⚽ Copa América: 2021, 2024

ACTIVITY AREAS

BENJAMIN PAVARD

Benjamin Pavard has matured into a technically brilliant defender. He has the ability to time his tackle perfectly and shut down opposing players in possession of the ball. He can also move the ball down one or two lines of defense with an incisive pass.

NATIONALITY
French

CURRENT CLUB
Inter Milan

28

DATE OF BIRTH	03/28/1996
POSITION	CENTER
HEIGHT	6 FT. 1 IN.
PRO DEBUT	2014
PREFERRED FOOT	RIGHT

APPEARANCES
257

BLOCKS
130

INTERCEPTIONS
437

AERIAL DUELS WON
61%

PENALTIES SCORED
0

PASS COMPLETION
88%

GOALS
11

PASSES
15,376

CLEARANCES
754

TACKLES
373

MAJOR CLUB HONORS
⊛ Serie A: 2024 ⊛ Bundesliga: 2020, 2021, 2022, 2023 (all B. Munich) ⊛ UEFA Champions League: 2020 (B. Munich) ⊛ UEFA Super Cup: 2020 (B. Munich) ⊛ FIFA Club World Cup: 2020 (B. Munich) ⊛ DFB-Pokal: 2020 (B. Munich)

INTERNATIONAL HONORS
⚽ FIFA World Cup: 2018, runner-up 2022
⊛ UEFA Nations League: 2021

ACTIVITY AREAS

NATIONALITY
Spanish

CURRENT CLUB
TBC

Very quick at anticipating danger, Sergio Ramos is a fine tackler with an excellent positional sense. Not only is he a skilled defender and great team leader, but is also known for regularly scoring important goals for his team. He left Sevilla after a season in 2024.

DATE OF BIRTH	03/30/1986
POSITION	CENTER
HEIGHT	6 FT. ¼ IN.
PRO DEBUT	2003
PREFERRED FOOT	RIGHT

BLOCKS
355

APPEARANCES
685

INTERCEPTIONS
1,361

AERIAL DUELS WON
67%

PENALTIES SCORED
19

PASS COMPLETION
88%

GOALS
96

PASSES
40,026

CLEARANCES
2,976

TACKLES
1,420

MAJOR CLUB HONORS

⚽ Ligue 1: 2022, 2023 (all PSG) ⚽ La Liga: 2007-08, 2012, 2017, 2020 (all R. Madrid) ⚽ UEFA Champions League: 2014, 2016, 2017, 2018 (all R. Madrid) ⚽ UEFA Super Cup: 2014, 2016, 2017 (all R. Madrid) ⚽ FIFA Club World Cup: 2014, 2016-18 (all R. Madrid)

INTERNATIONAL HONORS

⚽ FIFA World Cup: 2010
⚽ UEFA European Championship: 2008, 2012
⚽ FIFA Confederations Cup: Third place 2009, runner-up 2013

ACTIVITY AREAS

ANDREW ROBERTSON

NATIONALITY
Scottish

CURRENT CLUB
Liverpool

26

In a short space of time, Andrew Robertson has become one of the world's best left-side defenders. He is fast and an excellent tackler and reader of the game, plus his ability to hare down the flank, complete neat one-twos, and whip over dangerous crosses makes him an asset in attack.

DATE OF BIRTH	03/11/1994
POSITION	LEFT BACK
HEIGHT	5 FT. 10 IN.
PRO DEBUT	2012
PREFERRED FOOT	LEFT

APPEARANCES
330

BLOCKS
63

INTERCEPTIONS
303

AERIAL DUELS WON
52%

PENALTIES SCORED
0

PASS COMPLETION
84%

GOALS
12

PASSES
19,037

CLEARANCES
565

TACKLES
502

MAJOR CLUB HONORS
- Premier League: 2020
- UEFA Champions League: 2019
- FIFA World Club Cup: 2019
- UEFA Super Cup: 2019
- FA Cup: 2022

INTERNATIONAL HONORS
- None to date

ACTIVITY AREAS

22

NATIONALITY
German

CURRENT CLUB
Real Madrid

ANTONIO RÜDIGER

Antonio Rüdiger has become a dominant defender all along the back line, winning tackles with his strength and dominating the penalty area with his heading ability. He is also an excellent passer, reads the game well, and leads by example.

DATE OF BIRTH	03/03/1993
POSITION	CENTER
HEIGHT	6 FT. 2½ IN.
PRO DEBUT	2011
PREFERRED FOOT	RIGHT

BLOCKS 165

APPEARANCES 390

INTERCEPTIONS 378

AERIAL DUELS WON 59%

PASS COMPLETION 88%

PENALTIES SCORED 0

GOALS 17

PASSES 22,624

CLEARANCES 1,281

TACKLES 507

MAJOR CLUB HONORS
⚽ La Liga: 2024 ⚽ UEFA Champions League: 2021 (Chelsea), 2024 ⚽ FIFA World Club Cup: 2021 (Chelsea), 2022 ⚽ UEFA Europa League 2019 (Chelsea) ⚽ UEFA Super Cup: 2021 (Chelsea), 2022 ⚽ FA Cup: 2018 ⚽ Copa del Rey: 2023

INTERNATIONAL HONORS
⚽ FIFA Confederations Cup: 2017

ACTIVITY AREAS

STEFAN SAVIĆ

Stefan Savić reads the game well, but his biggest strength is his ability in the air. He is comfortable on the ball and neat with his short passing, relying on brains instead of brawn to operate effectively at the back.

NATIONALITY
Montenegran

CURRENT CLUB
Atlético Madrid

15

DATE OF BIRTH	01/08/1991
POSITION	CENTER
HEIGHT	6 FT. 1½ IN.
PRO DEBUT	2009
PREFERRED FOOT	RIGHT

APPEARANCES
385

BLOCKS
221

INTERCEPTIONS
666

AERIAL DUELS WON
64%

PENALTIES SCORED
0

PASS COMPLETION
85%

GOALS
8

PASSES
17,003

CLEARANCES
1,789

TACKLES
504

MAJOR CLUB HONORS
⚽ La Liga: 2021 ⚽ UEFA Champions League: Runner-up 2016 ⚽ UEFA Europa League: 2018 ⚽ UEFA Super Cup: 2018 ⚽ Premier League: 2012 (Man City)

INTERNATIONAL HONORS
⚽ None to date

ACTIVITY AREAS

NATIONALITY
Brazilian

CURRENT CLUB
Fluminense

THIAGO SILVA

Players past and present rate Thiago Silva as one of the best-ever center defenders to play the game. In addition to his technical strengths, he is a natural leader who can inspire teammates to lift their game in the heat of battle.

DATE OF BIRTH	09/22/1984
POSITION	CENTER
HEIGHT	6 FT.
PRO DEBUT	2002
PREFERRED FOOT	RIGHT

APPEARANCES
515

BLOCKS
358

INTERCEPTIONS
1.044

AERIAL DUELS WON
71%

PASS COMPLETION
93%

PENALTIES SCORED
0

GOALS
26

PASSES
34,404

CLEARANCES
2,590

TACKLES
743

MAJOR CLUB HONORS
⚽ UEFA Champions League: 2021 (Chelsea), runner-up 2020 (PSG) ⚽ UEFA Super Cup: 2021 (Chelsea) ⚽ FIFA Club World Cup: 2021 (Chelsea) ⚽ Serie A: 2011 (AC Milan) ⚽ Ligue 1: 2013-2020 (PSG) ⚽ Coupe de France: 2015-18, 2020 (all PSG) ⚽ FA Cup: 2022 (Chelsea)

INTERNATIONAL HONORS
⚽ FIFA Confederations Cup; 2013
⚽ Copa América: 2019, runner-up 2021

ACTIVITY AREAS

MILAN ŠKRINIAR

Centerback Milan Škriniar is a forceful tackler, strong in the air and combative on the ground. But what sets Škriniar apart are his ball-playing skills, being able to stay calm under pressure, and the ability to pick out intelligent passes.

NATIONALITY
Slovakian

CURRENT CLUB
Paris Saint-Germain

37

DATE OF BIRTH	02/11/1995
POSITION	CENTER
HEIGHT	6 FT. 1½ IN.
PRO DEBUT	2012
PREFERRED FOOT	RIGHT

APPEARANCES
296

BLOCKS
194

INTERCEPTIONS
263

AERIAL DUELS WON
51%

PASS COMPLETION
92%

PENALTIES SCORED
0

GOALS
12

PASSES
18,455

CLEARANCES
947

TACKLES
466

MAJOR CLUB HONORS
⚽ Ligue 1: 2024 ⚽ Serie A: 2021 (Inter Milan) ⚽ UEFA Champions League: Runner-up 2023 (Inter Milan) ⚽ UEFA Europa League: Runner-up 2020 (Inter Milan) ⚽ Coupe de France: 2024 ⚽ Coppa Italia: 2022, 2023 (Inter Milan)

INTERNATIONAL HONORS
⚽ King's Cup: 2018

ACTIVITY AREAS

2

NATIONALITY
French

CURRENT CLUB
Bayern Munich

DAYOT UPAMECANO

Dayot Upamecano has developed into an exceptional centerback with all the talents needed for the position. His standout talent is his ability with the ball at his feet— a quality that complements his passing accuracy.

DATE OF BIRTH	10/27/1998
POSITION	CENTER
HEIGHT	6 FT. 1 IN.
PRO DEBUT	2015
PREFERRED FOOT	RIGHT

BLOCKS
90

APPEARANCES
253

INTERCEPTIONS
365

PENALTIES SCORED
0

AERIAL DUELS WON
61%

PASS COMPLETION
88%

GOALS
6

PASSES
16,928

CLEARANCES
740

TACKLES
499

MAJOR CLUB HONORS
⚽ Bundesliga: 2022, 2023
⚽ DFL Supercup: 2021

INTERNATIONAL HONORS
⚽ UEFA Nations League: 2021
⚽ FIFA World Cup: Runner-up 2022

ACTIVITY AREAS

RAPHAËL VARANE

While most defenders peak in their late twenties, Raphaël Varane was already a star in his teens. Accurate with both feet, an excellent tackler, and great in the air, Varane can also launch attacks with his sharp passing and score goals. Varane left Manchester United in 2024 after three seasons.

NATIONALITY
French

CURRENT CLUB
TBC

DATE OF BIRTH	04/25/1993
POSITION	CENTER
HEIGHT	6 FT. 3 IN.
PRO DEBUT	2010
PREFERRED FOOT	RIGHT

BLOCKS
222

APPEARANCES
424

INTERCEPTIONS
565

PENALTIES SCORED
0

AERIAL DUELS WON
70%

PASS COMPLETION
88%

GOALS
14

PASSES
19,987

CLEARANCES
1,818

TACKLES
482

MAJOR CLUB HONORS
⚽ La Liga: 2012, 2017, 2020 (all R. Madrid) ⚽ UEFA Champions League: 2014, 2016, 2017, 2018 (all R. Madrid) ⚽ UEFA Super Cup: 2014, 2016, 2017 (all R. Madrid) ⚽ FIFA Club World Cup: 2014, 2016, 2017, 2018 (all R. Madrid) ⚽ FA Cup: Runner-up 2023, 2024 (Man. Utd)

INTERNATIONAL HONORS
⚽ FIFA World Cup: 2018, runner-up 2022
⚽ UEFA Nations League: 2021

ACTIVITY AREAS

MIDFIELDERS

Midfielders are the heartbeat of a team. Not only do they play between the forwards and the defenders but they also help their teammates at both ends. Midfielders fall into one of four main categories: 1.) defensive midfielders who sit in front of the back four and are great tacklers; 2.) the attacking fullbacks operating on the wings who whip crosses into the box; 3.) the center midfielders who are great at setting up and then joining attacks, as well as helping out in defense whenever needed; 4.) the playmakers—these are the stars who build the attack with their creative play.

WHAT DO THE STATS MEAN?

ASSISTS
A pass, cross, or header to a teammate who then scores counts as an assist. This stat also includes a deflected shot that is converted by a teammate.

SHOTS
Any deliberate strike on goal counts as a shot. The strike does not have to be on target or force a save from the keeper.

CHANCES CREATED
Any pass that results in a shot at goal (whether or not the goal is scored) is regarded as a chance created.

TACKLES
This is the number of times the player has challenged and dispossessed the opposition without committing a foul.

DRIBBLES
This is the number of times the player has gone past an opponent while running with the ball.

75%
SUCCESSFUL PASSES
This shows as a percentage how successful the midfielder is at finding teammates with passes, whether from 5 or 60 yards.

Did you know?

In top-level soccer, midfielders tend to cover the most ground during the course of a match. A midfielder playing the full 90 minutes will usually run anywhere between 6 and 7 1/2 miles.

NATIONALITY
English

CURRENT CLUB
Real Madrid

JUDE BELLINGHAM

Jude Bellingham's talent was evident when he was just 16 years old! Now he has fulfilled that promise and become one of the world's best midfielders playing for one of world's best clubs. He is a good tackler, exceptionally quick, positionally aware, and able to create and score goals.

DATE OF BIRTH	06/29/2003
POSITION	CENTER
HEIGHT	6 FT. 1 IN.
PRO DEBUT	2019
PREFERRED FOOT	RIGHT

PENALTIES SCORED
2

APPEARANCES
156

DRIBBLES
485

ASSISTS
32

PASSES
7247
SUCCESSFUL PASSES
85%

SHOTS
271

GOALS
43

CHANCES CREATED
184

TACKLES
296

MAJOR CLUB HONORS
⚽ La Liga: 2024
⚽ UEFA Champions League: 2024
⚽ Bundesliga: Runner-up 2023 (Borussia Dortmund)
⚽ DFB-Pokal: 2021 (Borussia Dortmund)

INTERNATIONAL HONORS
⚽ UEFA European Championship: Runner-up 2020 (2021), runner-up 2024

ACTIVITY AREAS

KEVIN DE BRUYNE

Kevin De Bruyne ranks as one of the finest attacking midfielders in the game today. Strong and technically brilliant, he can break up play at one end and almost immediately blast a 25-yard shot into the opposite goal. In 2024, he notched up his 100th goal for Manchester City.

NATIONALITY
Belgian

CURRENT CLUB
Manchester City

17

DATE OF BIRTH	06/28/1991
POSITION	ATTACKING
HEIGHT	5 FT. 11¼ IN.
PRO DEBUT	2008
PREFERRED FOOT	RIGHT

APPEARANCES
428

ASSISTS
177

DRIBBLES
1,249

PASSES
20,607
SUCCESSFUL PASSES
81%

PENALTIES SCORED
5

GOALS
112

SHOTS
1,035

CHANCES CREATED
1,246

TACKLES
508

MAJOR CLUB HONORS
⚽ Premier League: 2018, 2019, 2021, 2022, 2023, 2024
⚽ UEFA Champions League: Runner-up 2021, 2023
⚽ FA Cup: 2019, 2023

INTERNATIONAL HONORS
⚽ FIFA World Cup: Third place 2018

ACTIVITY AREAS

5

NATIONALITY
Spanish

CURRENT CLUB
Inter Miami

SERGIO BUSQUETS

Sergio Busquets plays as a deep midfielder who dictates the team's build-up play with smart short and longer passes. He is great at stopping attacks before they become dangerous and then making passes to launch his team's raids.

DATE OF BIRTH	07/16/1988
POSITION	DEFENSIVE
HEIGHT	6 FT. 2¼ IN.
PRO DEBUT	2007
PREFERRED FOOT	RIGHT

APPEARANCES
645

ASSISTS
45

DRIBBLES
441

PENALTIES SCORED
0

PASSES
46,099
SUCCESSFUL PASSES
91%

GOALS
17

SHOTS
155

CHANCES CREATED
417

TACKLES
1,650

MAJOR CLUB HONORS

⚽ La Liga: 2009-11, 2013, 2015 2016, 2018, 2019, 2023 (All Barça)
⚽ UEFA Champions League: 2009, 2011, 2015 (all Barça) ⚽ UEFA Super Cup: 2009, 2011, 2015 (all Barça) ⚽ FIFA Club World Cup: 2009, 2011, 2015 (all Barça) ⚽ MLS Leagues Cup: 2023

INTERNATIONAL HONORS

⚽ FIFA World Cup: 2010 ⚽ UEFA European Championship: 2012 ⚽ FIFA Confederations Cup: Runner up 2013 ⚽ UEFA Nations League: Runner-up 2021

ACTIVITY AREAS

EMRE CAN

Having been a defender earlier in his career, Emre Can has grown into a classy center midfielder. He combines his excellent tackling strength with his midfielder's instincts to thread passes to teammates in attacking positions.

NATIONALITY
German

CURRENT CLUB
Borussia Dortmund

23

DATE OF BIRTH	01/12/1994
POSITION	CENTER
HEIGHT	6 FT. 1 IN.
PRO DEBUT	2011
PREFERRED FOOT	RIGHT

APPEARANCES
369

ASSISTS
20

DRIBBLES
615

PENALTIES SCORED
8

PASSES
18,346
SUCCESSFUL PASSES
85%

GOALS
32

SHOTS
327

CHANCES CREATED
235

TACKLES
802

MAJOR CLUB HONORS

⚽ Bundesliga: 2013 (B. Munich), runner-up 2023 ⚽ UEFA Champions League: 2013 (B. Munich), runner-up 2018 (Liverpool), runner-up 2024 ⚽ UEFA Europa League: runner-up 2016 (Liverpool) ⚽ Serie A: 2019, 2020 (Juventus) ⚽ DFB-Pokal: 2013 (B. Munich) 2021

INTERNATIONAL HONORS

⚽ FIFA Confederations Cup: 2017

ACTIVITY AREAS

18

NATIONALITY
Brazilian

CURRENT CLUB
Manchester United

CASEMIRO

Casemiro's strengths are his great energy, high work rate, and good support play. Strong, mobile, and hard-tackling, his best position is as a defensive midfielder, but his mobility helps him get from box to box and he can also play at centerback.

DATE OF BIRTH	02/23/1992
POSITION	CENTER
HEIGHT	6 FT. ¾ IN.
PRO DEBUT	2010
PREFERRED FOOT	RIGHT

ASSISTS
28

APPEARANCES
370

DRIBBLES
271

PASSES
19,756
SUCCESSFUL PASSES
85%

PENALTIES SCORED
0

GOALS
38

SHOTS
429

CHANCES CREATED
236

TACKLES
1,127

MAJOR CLUB HONORS

⚽ La Liga: 2017, 2020, 2022 (all R. Madrid) ⚽ UEFA Champs League: 2014, 2016, 2017, 2018, 2022 (all R. Madrid) ⚽ UEFA Super Cup: 2016, 2017, 2022 (all R. Madrid) ⚽ FIFA Club World Cup: 2016, 2017, 2018 (all R. Madrid) ⚽ FA Cup: Runner-up 2023, 2024

INTERNATIONAL HONORS

⚽ FIFA U-20 World Cup: 2011
⚽ Copa América: 2019, runner-up 2021

ACTIVITY AREAS

ALPHONSO DAVIES

Ghana-born Alphonso Davies is already considered one of the finest male soccer players to represent Canada. He is equally productive and confident at all left-side positions, thanks to his great pace, dribbling talent, passing creativity, stamina, and crossing ability.

NATIONALITY
Canadian

CURRENT CLUB
Bayern Munich

19

DATE OF BIRTH	11/02/2000
POSITION	LEFT WING
HEIGHT	6 FT. 3/4 IN.
PRO DEBUT	2016
PREFERRED FOOT	LEFT

APPEARANCES
241

DRIBBLES
1,142

ASSISTS
36

PASSES
9,723

SUCCESSFUL PASSES
86%

GOALS
17

PENALTIES SCORED
0

SHOTS
153

CHANCES CREATED
267

TACKLES
414

MAJOR CLUB HONORS
⚽ Bundesliga: 2019, 2020, 2021, 2022, 2023 ⚽ UEFA Champions League: 2020 ⚽ FIFA Club World Cup 2020 ⚽ UEFA Super Cup: 2020 ⚽ DFB-Pokal: 2019, 2020

INTERNATIONAL HONORS
⚽ None to date

ACTIVITY AREAS

10

NATIONALITY
French

CURRENT CLUB
Paris Saint-Germain

OUSMANE DEMBÉLÉ

Ousmane Dembélé's speed, dribbling skills, and ability to take on defenders make him a natural winger. Capable of playing on either flank, he frequently uses his pace and technical skills to create goal-scoring opportunities for himself or provide key passes and assists to his teammates.

DATE OF BIRTH	05/15/1997
POSITION	WINGER
HEIGHT	5 FT. 10 IN.
PRO DEBUT	2014
PREFERRED FOOT	BOTH

ASSISTS
71

APPEARANCES
268

DRIBBLES
1,348

PENALTIES SCORED
2

PASSES
7,936
SUCCESSFUL PASSES
80%

GOALS
57

SHOTS
489

CHANCES CREATED
464

TACKLES
208

MAJOR CLUB HONORS
⚽ Ligue 1: 2024 ⚽ La Liga: 2018, 2019, 2023 (all Barcelona) ⚽ Coupe de France: 2024 ⚽ Copa del Rey: 2018, 2021 (all Barcelona) ⚽ DFB Pokal: 2017 (Borussia Dortmund)

INTERNATIONAL HONORS
⚽ FIFA World Cup: 2018, runner-up 2022

ACTIVITY AREAS

BRUNO FERNANDES

Bruno Fernandes shines as a center or attacking midfielder. A sound defensive player, he has a fantastic eye for creating chances with through balls, driving powerful shots from long range, and is superb with penalties and freekicks.

NATIONALITY
Portuguese

CURRENT CLUB
Manchester United

8

DATE OF BIRTH	09/08/1994
POSITION	ATTACKING
HEIGHT	5 FT. 10¼ IN.
PRO DEBUT	2012
PREFERRED FOOT	RIGHT

APPEARANCES
347*

ASSISTS
79

DRIBBLES
595

PENALTIES SCORED
31

PASSES
15,146
SUCCESSFUL PASSES
77%

GOALS
96

SHOTS
852

CHANCES CREATED
775

TACKLES
534

*Excludes data from Portuguese Premeira League

MAJOR CLUB HONORS
⚽ UEFA Europa League: Runner-up 2021 ⚽ Taça de Portugal: 2019 (Sporting CP) ⚽ Taça de Liga: 2018, 2019 (Sporting CP) ⚽ FA Cup: Runner-up 2023, 2024

INTERNATIONAL HONORS
⚽ UEFA Nations League: 2019

ACTIVITY AREAS

8

NATIONALITY
Argentinian

CURRENT CLUB
Chelsea

ENZO FERNÁNDEZ

Enzo Fernandez has enjoyed a meteoric rise, highlighted by his award as FIFA Best Young Player at the 2022 World Cup. Playing in center midfield, he is happy to help his defenders, while his exceptionally accurate long-range passing often launches dangerous attacks.

DATE OF BIRTH	01/17/2001
POSITION	CENTER
HEIGHT	5 FT. 10 IN.
PRO DEBUT	2019
PREFERRED FOOT	RIGHT

ASSISTS
5

APPEARANCES
55*

DRIBBLES
87

PENALTIES
SCORED
1

PASSES
3,804
SUCCESSFUL
PASSES
88%

GOALS
3

SHOTS
86

CHANCES
CREATED
58

TACKLES
122

*Excludes data
from Argentine and
Portuguese Leagues

MAJOR CLUB HONORS
⚽ Argentina Primera División: 2021 (River Plate)

INTERNATIONAL HONORS
⚽ FIFA World Cup: 2022
⚽ Copa América: 2024

ACTIVITY AREAS

YOUSSOUF FOFANA

A commanding presence in the middle of the park, Youssouf Fofana plays a key role for both club and country. He is known for his box-to-box presence and is comfortable taking a leadership role, orchestrating the play and controlling the tempo of the match.

NATIONALITY
French

CURRENT CLUB
Monaco

19

DATE OF BIRTH	01/10/1999
POSITION	CENTER
HEIGHT	6 FT. ¾ IN.
PRO DEBUT	2017
PREFERRED FOOT	RIGHT

APPEARANCES
186

ASSISTS
16

DRIBBLES
380

PASSES
7,941
SUCCESSFUL PASSES
82%

PENALTIES SCORED
0

GOALS
10

SHOTS
211

CHANCES CREATED
148

TACKLES
394

MAJOR CLUB HONORS
 ⚽ Coupe De La Ligue: 2019

INTERNATIONAL HONORS
⚽ FIFA World Cup: Runner-up 2022

ACTIVITY AREAS

10

NATIONALITY
English

CURRENT CLUB
Manchester City

JACK GREALISH

Jack Grealish is among the finest attacking midfielders in Europe. He displays tight ball control, dribbling ability, change of speed, and can shoot or deliver dangerous balls into the penalty area from the right or center positions.

DATE OF BIRTH	10/09/1995
POSITION	ATTACKING
HEIGHT	5 FT. 9 IN.
PRO DEBUT	2013
PREFERRED FOOT	RIGHT

APPEARANCES
198

ASSISTS
32

DRIBBLES
576

PASSES
6,501
SUCCESSFUL PASSES
87%

PENALTIES SCORED
0

GOALS
27

SHOTS
299

CHANCES CREATED
395

TACKLES
152

MAJOR CLUB HONORS
⚽ Premier League: 2022, 2023, 2024 ⚽ UEFA Champions League: 2023 ⚽ FA Cup: Runner-up 2015 (Aston Villa), 2023, runner-up 2024

INTERNATIONAL HONORS
⚽ UEFA European Championship: Runner-up 2020 (2021)

ACTIVITY AREAS

44

İLKAY GÜNDOĞAN

Although İlkay Gündoğan became a superstar relatively late in his career, his teammates have always recognized his value. Admired for his solid defensive talent, great energy, passing ability, and reading situations, he has developed a knack for scoring vital goals.

NATIONALITY
German

CURRENT CLUB
Barcelona

22

DATE OF BIRTH	10/24/1990
POSITION	CENTER
HEIGHT	5 FT. 10¾ IN.
PRO DEBUT	2008
PREFERRED FOOT	RIGHT

APPEARANCES
479

ASSISTS
56

DRIBBLES
881

PASSES
26,868
SUCCESSFUL PASSES
89%

PENALTIES SCORED
5

GOALS
76

SHOTS
692

CHANCES CREATED
611

TACKLES
617

MAJOR CLUB HONORS
⚽ UEFA Champions League: 2023 (Man. City), runner-up 2021 (Man. City), runner-up 2013 (B. Dortmund) ⚽ Premier League: 2018, 2019, 2021-23 (all Man. City) ⚽ Bundesliga: 2012 (B. Dortmund) ⚽ FA Cup: 2018, 2019 (Man City) ⚽ DFB-Pokal: 2012 (B. Dortmund)

INTERNATIONAL HONORS
⚽ None to date

ACTIVITY AREAS

21

NATIONALITY
Dutch

CURRENT CLUB
Barcelona

FRENKIE DE JONG

Frenkie de Jong has been an outstanding talent ever since he burst onto the scene as a teenager. His close control, work rate, passing accuracy, and movement have seen him being compared to the great Johan Cruyff.

DATE OF BIRTH	05/12/1997
POSITION	CENTER
HEIGHT	5 FT. 10¾ IN.
PRO DEBUT	2015
PREFERRED FOOT	RIGHT

ASSISTS
26

APPEARANCES
264

DRIBBLES
509

PENALTIES SCORED
0

PASSES
17,007
SUCCESSFUL PASSES
92%

GOALS
17

SHOTS
126

CHANCES CREATED
309

TACKLES
375

MAJOR CLUB HONORS

⚽ La Liga: 2023 ⚽ UEFA Europa League: Runner-up 2017 (Ajax) ⚽ Copa del Rey: 2021 ⚽ Eredivisie: 2019 (Ajax) ⚽ KNVB Cup: 2019 (Ajax)

INTERNATIONAL HONORS

⚽ UEFA Nations League: Runner-up: 2019

ACTIVITY AREAS

JORGINHO

The talented Jorginho can control the tempo of play from deep as he links defense with midfield and midfield with attack with his accurate passing. He has the awareness, vision, and passing ability to break lines and can deliver lofted balls to attacking teammates.

NATIONALITY
Italian

CURRENT CLUB
Arsenal

20

DATE OF BIRTH	12/20/1991
POSITION	DEFENSIVE
HEIGHT	5 FT. 10¾ IN.
PRO DEBUT	2010
PREFERRED FOOT	BOTH

APPEARANCES
402

ASSISTS
28

DRIBBLES
291

PASSES
28,305
SUCCESSFUL PASSES
89%

PENALTIES SCORED
33

GOALS
38

SHOTS
173

CHANCES CREATED
394

TACKLES
799

MAJOR CLUB HONORS

⚽ Premier League: Runner-up 2023, runner-up 2024 ⚽ UEFA Champs League: 2021 (Chelsea) ⚽ UEFA Europa League: 2019 (Chelsea) ⚽ FIFA World Club Cup: 2021 (Chelsea) ⚽ UEFA Super Cup: 2021 (Chelsea) ⚽ FA Cup: Runner-up 2020-22 (Chelsea) ⚽ Coppa Italia: 2014 (Napoli)

INTERNATIONAL HONORS

⚽ UEFA European Championship: 2020
⚽ UEFA Nations League: Third place 2021, third place 2023

ACTIVITY AREAS

NATIONALITY
German

CURRENT CLUB
Retired in 2024

TONI KROOS

A set-piece specialist who wins challenges in both boxes and dictates the game, Toni Kroos is an athletic box-to-box midfielder who can can pass long and short with either foot. He possesses great vision, creativit,y and energy.

DATE OF BIRTH	01/04/1990
POSITION	CENTER
HEIGHT	6 FT.
PRO DEBUT	2007
PREFERRED FOOT	RIGHT

ASSISTS
129

APPEARANCES
630

DRIBBLES
649

PASSES
40,899
SUCCESSFUL
PASSES
92%

PENALTIES
SCORED
0

GOALS
56

SHOTS
890

CHANCES
CREATED
1,281

TACKLES
1,160

MAJOR CLUB HONORS

⚽ La Liga: 2017, 2020, 2022, 2024 (all R. Madrid) ⚽ Bundesliga: 2008, 2013, '14 (all B. Munich) ⚽ UEFA Champs League.: 2013 (B. Munich), 2016, '17, '18, '22, '24 (all R.Madrid) ⚽ FIFA Club WC: 2013 (B. Munich), 2014,'16, '17 '18, 2022 ⚽ UEFA Super Cup: 2013 (B. Mun.), 2014, '17, '22 (all R. Mad.)

INTERNATIONAL HONORS

⚽ FIFA World Cup: 2014

ACTIVITY AREAS

LUKA MODRIĆ

A top player for more than 20 years and a former Ballon d'Or winner (2018), Luka Modrić is still capable of determining the outcome of a match. He has a great soccer-playing brain, can deliver long and short passes with both feet, and can strike powerful long-range shots, especially free kicks.

NATIONALITY
Croatian

CURRENT CLUB
Real Madrid

10

DATE OF BIRTH	09/09/1985
POSITION	ATTACKING
HEIGHT	5 FT. 7½ IN.
PRO DEBUT	2003
PREFERRED FOOT	RIGHT

APPEARANCES
616

ASSISTS
90

DRIBBLES
1,451

PENALTIES SCORED
5

PASSES
34,352
SUCCESSFUL PASSES
89%

GOALS
51

SHOTS
728

CHANCES CREATED
964

TACKLES
790

MAJOR CLUB HONORS
⚽ La Liga: 2017, 2020, 2022, runner-up 2023, 2024 ⚽ UEFA Champions League: 2014, 2016, 2017, 2018, 2022, 2024 ⚽ UEFA Super Cup: 2014, 2016, 2017, 2022 ⚽ FIFA Club World Cup: 2014, 2016, 2017, 2018, 2022 ⚽ Copa del Rey: 2023

INTERNATIONAL HONORS
⚽ FIFA World Cup: Runner-up 2018, third place 2022
⚽ UEFA Nations League: Runner-up 2023

ACTIVITY AREAS

25

NATIONALITY
German

CURRENT CLUB
Bayern Munich

THOMAS MÜLLER

Thomas Müller is a dangerous attacking midfielder who scores countless goals playing just behind a lone striker. The German powerhouse is mentally strong, tactically clever, and great at finding holes in the opposition's defense.

DATE OF BIRTH	09/13/1989
POSITION	SECOND STRIKER
HEIGHT	6 FT. ¾ IN.
PRO DEBUT	2008
PREFERRED FOOT	RIGHT

ASSISTS
193

APPEARANCES
624

DRIBBLES
1,046

PASSES
20,004

SUCCESSFUL PASSES
77%

PENALTIES SCORED
22

GOALS
203

SHOTS
1,196

CHANCES CREATED
1,168

TACKLES
645

MAJOR CLUB HONORS

⚽ Bundesliga: 2010, 2013, 2014, 2015, 2016, 2017, 2018, 2019, 2020, 2021, 2022, 2023 ⚽ DFB-Pokal: 2010, 2013, 2014, 2016, 2019, 2020 ⚽ UEFA Champions League: Runner-up 2010, runner-up 2012, 2013, 2020 ⚽ FIFA Club World Cup: 2013, 2020

INTERNATIONAL HONORS

⚽ FIFA World Cup: 2014, third place 2010

ACTIVITY AREAS

CHRISTIAN PULISIC

Although capable of playing in any attacking position, Christian Pulisic's pace, agility, and technical ability have made him most effective on the left wing. He also likes to have the ball at his feet, dribbling past opponents to create shooting opportunities for himself.

NATIONALITY
American

CURRENT CLUB
AC Milan

11

DATE OF BIRTH	09/18/1998
POSITION	RIGHT
HEIGHT	5 FT. 10¼ IN.
PRO DEBUT	2016
PREFERRED FOOT	BOTH

APPEARANCES
290

ASSISTS
41

DRIBBLES
1,142

PASSES
6,439

SUCCESSFUL PASSES
80%

PENALTIES SCORED
0

GOALS
55

SHOTS
409

CHANCES CREATED
277

TACKLES
256

MAJOR CLUB HONORS
⚽ UEFA Champions League: 2021 (Chelsea) ⚽ UEFA Super Cup: 2021 (Chelsea) ⚽ FIFA Club World Cup: 2021 (Chelsea)
⚽ DFB-Pokal: 2017 (Borussia Dortmund)

INTERNATIONAL HONORS
⚽ CONCACAF Nations League: 2020
⚽ ONCACAF Gold Cup: Runner-up 2019

ACTIVITY AREAS

41

NATIONALITY
English

CURRENT CLUB
Arsenal

DECLAN RICE

Declan Rice has long been considered an exceptional defensive midfielder; now he has found an attacking flair playing in center midfield. He has added fine ball skills, passing, crossing, and long-range shooting to his athleticism and tackling ability.

DATE OF BIRTH	01/14/1999
POSITION	RIGHT
HEIGHT	6 FT. 1 IN.
PRO DEBUT	2017
PREFERRED FOOT	RIGHT

ASSISTS
20

APPEARANCES
273

DRIBBLES
375

PENALTIES SCORED
1

PASSES
13,405
SUCCESSFUL PASSES
88%

GOALS
21

SHOTS
230

CHANCES CREATED
185

TACKLES
608

MAJOR CLUB HONORS
⚽ Premier League: Runner-up 2024
⚽ UEFA Europa Conference League: 2023 (West Ham Utd)

INTERNATIONAL HONORS
⚽ UEFA European Championship: Runner-up 2020 (2021), runner-up 2024
⚽ UEFA Nations League: (third place) 2019

ACTIVITY AREAS

BUKAYO SAKA

A rising star in world soccer, Buyako Saka's versatility is just one of his talents. Equally good on both sides at fullback or winger, his creativity, positional sense, tackling, shooting, and passing talents are displayed best as a right midfielder.

NATIONALITY
English

CURRENT CLUB
Arsenal

DATE OF BIRTH	09/05/2001
POSITION	WINGER
HEIGHT	5 FT. 10 IN.
PRO DEBUT	2018
PREFERRED FOOT	LEFT

APPEARANCES
204

ASSISTS
47

DRIBBLES
633

PENALTIES SCORED
10

PASSES
6,142
SUCCESSFUL PASSES
82%

GOALS
56

SHOTS
419

CHANCES CREATED
345

TACKLES
268

MAJOR CLUB HONORS
⚽ Premier League: Runner-up 2023, runner-up 2024
⚽ FA Cup: 2020
⚽ UEFA Europa League: Runner-up 2019

INTERNATIONAL HONORS
⚽ UEFA European Championship: Runner-up 2020 (2021), runner-up 2024

ACTIVITY AREAS

10

NATIONALITY
German

CURRENT CLUB
Bayern Munich

LEROY SANÉ

Leroy Sané is almost the perfect example of a right winger, except his left foot is stronger. He has all the other attributes to be fearsome on the flanks: great ball control, fine positional and tactical sense, top-class dribbling, and outstanding pace to beat defenders.

DATE OF BIRTH	01/11/1996
POSITION	WINGER
HEIGHT	6 FT.
PRO DEBUT	2014
PREFERRED FOOT	LEFT

ASSISTS
85

APPEARANCES
327

DRIBBLES
1,513

PENALTIES SCORED
0

PASSES
9,102
SUCCESSFUL PASSES
83%

GOALS
88

SHOTS
682

CHANCES CREATED
463

TACKLES
343

MAJOR CLUB HONORS
⚽ Bundesliga: 2021, 2022, 2023 ⚽ FIFA Club World Cup: 2020 2021 ⚽ UEFA Super Cup: 2020 ⚽ Premier League: 2018, 2019 (all Man. City) ⚽ FA Cup: 2019 (Man. City)

INTERNATIONAL HONORS
⚽ FIFA Confederations Cup: 2017

ACTIVITY AREAS

GEORGINIO WIJNALDUM

Georginio Wijnaldum can play anywhere in the middle of the field as an attacking playmaker or a defensive shield for the back line. Good with both feet and a strong tackler, he goes box to box and scores crucial goals, especially with headers.

NATIONALITY
Dutch

CURRENT CLUB
Al-Ittefaq

25

DATE OF BIRTH	11/11/1990
POSITION	CENTER
HEIGHT	5 FT. 9 IN.
PRO DEBUT	2007
PREFERRED FOOT	RIGHT

ASSISTS
48

APPEARANCES
589

DRIBBLES
1,075

PASSES
18,310

PENALTIES SCORED
6

SUCCESSFUL PASSES
88%

GOALS
113

SHOTS
776

CHANCES CREATED
458

TACKLES
464

MAJOR CLUB HONORS
⚽ Ligue 1: 2022 (PSG) ⚽ Premier League: 2020 (Liv'pool)
⚽ UEFA Champions League: 2019 (Liv'pool), runner-up 2018 (Liv'pool) ⚽ Europa League: Runner-up 2023 (Roma) ⚽ UEFA Super Cup: 2019 (Liv'pool) ⚽ FIFA Club World Cup: 2019 (Liv'pool)

INTERNATIONAL HONORS
⚽ UEFA Nations League: Runner-up: 2019
⚽ FIFA World Cup: Third place 2014

ACTIVITY AREAS

20

NATIONALITY
Belgian

CURRENT CLUB
Atlético Madrid

AXEL WITSEL

Originally a face-pace right winger, Axel Witsel has developed into a strong center midfielder. He frequently drives his team forward with both his play and leadership skills. He is especially good at delivering dangerous passes with either foot.

DATE OF BIRTH	01/12/1989
POSITION	CENTER
HEIGHT	6 FT. 1 IN.
PRO DEBUT	2006
PREFERRED FOOT	RIGHT

ASSISTS
11

APPEARANCES
278

DRIBBLES
217

PENALTIES
SCORED
1

PASSES
15,193
SUCCESSFUL
PASSES
92%

GOALS
21

SHOTS
205

CHANCES
CREATED
108

TACKLES
408

MAJOR CLUB HONORS
⚽ DFL-Pokal: 2021 (Borussia Dortmund)
⚽ DFL-Supercup: 2019 (Borussia Dortmund)

INTERNATIONAL HONORS
⚽ FIFA World Cup: Third place 2018

ACTIVITY AREAS

GRANIT XHAKA

Granit Xhaka makes any team he plays for much harder to break down with his performances in defensive midfield. One of the fittest players around, he combines boundless energy with great positional sense and fine tackling technique, and opponents must respect his long-range shooting ability.

NATIONALITY
Swiss

CURRENT CLUB
Bayer Leverkusen

34

DATE OF BIRTH	09/27/1992
POSITION	DEFENSIVE
HEIGHT	6 FT. 1 IN.
PRO DEBUT	2010
PREFERRED FOOT	LEFT

ASSISTS
34

APPEARANCES
451

DRIBBLES
472

PENALTIES SCORED
1

PASSES
30,993
SUCCESSFUL PASSES
88%

GOALS
32

SHOTS
501

CHANCES CREATED
443

TACKLES
798

MAJOR CLUB HONORS
⚽ Bundesliga: 2024 ⚽ DFB-Pokal: 2024 ⚽ FA Cup: 2017, 2020 (Arsenal) ⚽ Swiss Super League: 2011, 2012 (all Basel)

INTERNATIONAL HONORS
⚽ None to date

ACTIVITY AREAS

FORWARDS

The forwards are a team's frontline attackers and the chief goal scorers. They are also the team's most celebrated players. Whether it is the smaller, quicker player, such as Neymar and Mohamed Salah, or the bigger, more physical attacker, such as Erling Haaland and Romelu Lukaku, strikers have perfected the art of finding the back of the net on a regular basis. Aside from scoring a lot of goals, the world's best strikers are also effective at creating chances for their teammates.

WHAT DO THE STATS MEAN?

GOALS
This is the total number of goals a striker has scored. The figure spans across all the top clubs the player has represented so far in his career.

75%

CONVERSION RATE
The percentage shows how good the player is at taking a chance in front of goal. If a player scores two goals from four shots, his conversion rate is 50 percent.

ASSISTS
A pass, cross, or header to a teammate who then scores counts as an assist. This stat also includes a deflected shot that is immediately converted by a teammate.

128

MINUTES PER GOAL
This is the average length of time it takes for the player to score. It is calculated across all the minutes the player has played in his career at top level.

9

NATIONALITY
French

CURRENT CLUB
Al-Ittihad

KARIM BENZEMA

Karim Benzema, now playing in Saudi Arabia, is an intelligent forward with a great work rate, who can play out wide, down the middle, or behind the front man. Although right-footed, he creates and scores goals with his left and his head.

DATE OF BIRTH	12/19/1987
POSITION	STRIKER
HEIGHT	6 FT. ¾ IN.
PRO DEBUT	2004
PREFERRED FOOT	BOTH

GOALS
380

PENALTIES SCORED
33

ASSISTS
150

APPEARANCES
718

SHOT CONVERSION
18%

MINUTES PER GOAL
137

GOALS LEFT
70

GOALS RIGHT
246

HAT TRICKS
11

HEADED GOALS
59

SHOTS
2,105

MAJOR CLUB HONORS

⚽ La Liga: 2012, '17, '20, '22 (R. Madrid) ⚽ UEFA Champions League: 2014, '16, '17, '18, '22 (R. Madrid) ⚽ FIFA Club World Cup: 2014, '16, '17, '18, '22 (R. Madrid) ⚽ UEFA Super Cup: 2014, '16, '17, '22 (R. Madrid) ⚽ Ligue 1: 2005, '06, '07, '08 (Lyon) ⚽ Copa del Rey: 2023 (R. Madrid)

INTERNATIONAL HONORS

⚽ UEFA Nations League: 2021
⚽ FIFA World Cup: Runner-up 2022

ACTIVITY AREAS

JONATHAN DAVID

Jonathan David is a live wire on the field who combines speed, balance, and excellent ball control. Normally used as second striker, feeding off a target man, he finds holes in opposing defenses, through which he can run or deliver inch-perfect passes.

NATIONALITY
Canadian

CURRENT CLUB
Lille

9

DATE OF BIRTH	14/01/2000
POSITION	STRIKER
HEIGHT	5 FT. 9 IN.
PRO DEBUT	2018
PREFERRED FOOT	201BOTH

GOALS
77

PENALTIES SCORED
16

APPEARANCES
162

ASSISTS
10

SHOT CONVERSION
22%

MINUTES PER GOAL
158

GOALS LEFT
24

GOALS RIGHT
48

HAT TRICKS
2

HEADED GOALS
5

SHOTS
343

MAJOR CLUB HONORS
⚽ Ligue 1: 2021

INTERNATIONAL HONORS
⚽ None to date

ACTIVITY AREAS

61

NATIONALITY
Dutch

CURRENT CLUB
TBC

MEMPHIS DEPAY

Memphis Depay has developed into a world-class striker, although he is still considered to be a left winger or left-side striker. He is a brave player and will challenge the biggest defenders in the middle of the danger area. Depay left Atlético Madrid in 2024 after a single season.

DATE OF BIRTH	02/13/1994
POSITION	WINGER
HEIGHT	5 FT. 10 IN.
PRO DEBUT	2011
PREFERRED FOOT	RIGHT

GOALS
135

PENALTIES SCORED
20

ASSISTS
67

APPEARANCES
354

SHOT CONVERSION
13%

MINUTES PER GOAL
171

GOALS LEFT
24

GOALS RIGHT
105

HAT TRICKS
3

HEADED GOALS
6

SHOTS
1,024

MAJOR CLUB HONORS
⚽ Eredivisie: 2015 (PSV Eindhoven) ⚽ KNVB Cup: 2012 (PSV Eindhoven) ⚽ FA Cup: 2016 (Manchester United)

INTERNATIONAL HONORS
⚽ FIFA World Cup: Third place 2014

ACTIVITY AREAS

JOÃO FÉLIX

Portugal's João Félix perfected his craft in *La Liga*, where he has now returned following a loan spell in the Premier League in 2023. An eye for goal combined with versatility mean he can be deployed as a center striker, second forward, attacking midfielder, or winger.

NATIONALITY
Portuguese

CURRENT CLUB
Barcelona (on loan)

14

DATE OF BIRTH	11/10/1999
POSITION	FORWARD
HEIGHT	5 FT. 11¼ IN.
PRO DEBUT	2016
PREFERRED FOOT	RIGHT

GOALS
46

PENALTIES SCORED
3

APPEARANCES
183

ASSISTS
19

SHOT CONVERSION
13%

MINUTES PER GOAL
225

GOALS LEFT
9

GOALS RIGHT
32

HAT TRICKS
0

HEADED GOALS
5

SHOTS
368

MAJOR CLUB HONORS
- ⚽ La Liga: 2021 (Atlético Madrid)
- ⚽ Primeira Liga: 2019 (Benfica)

INTERNATIONAL HONORS
- ⚽ UEFA Nations League: 2019

ACTIVITY AREAS

47

NATIONALITY
English

CURRENT CLUB
Manchester City

PHIL FODEN

Phil Foden's meteoric rise may see him become one of the world's best players. Left-footed, he plays on either wing or in the center as a striker or midfielder, where he displays an exceptional first touch, close control, poise, balance, tactical awareness, and a powerful shot.

DATE OF BIRTH	28/05/2000
POSITION	SECOND STRIKER
HEIGHT	1.71 M
PRO DEBUT	2016
PREFERRED FOOT	LEFT

GOALS
69

PENALTIES SCORED
0

ASSISTS
37

APPEARANCES
216

SHOT CONVERSION
17%

MINUTES PER GOAL
190

GOALS LEFT
51

GOALS RIGHT
15

HAT TRICKS
3

HEADED GOALS
3

SHOTS
412

MAJOR CLUB HONORS
⚽ Premier League: 2018, 2019, 2021, 2022, 2023, 2024 ⚽ UEFA Champions League: 2023, runners-up 2021 ⚽ UEFA Super Cup: 2023 ⚽ FIFA Club World Cup: 2023 ⚽ FA Cup: 2019, 2023, runner-up 2024

INTERNATIONAL HONORS
⚽ UEFA European Championship: Runner-up 2024

ACTIVITY AREAS

OLIVIER GIROUD

Olivier Giroud is much more than a target man, because his work rate and positional sense make him hard to defend against near the goal. He uses his physique to hold and shield the ball, and is known for his accurate passing, shooting, and heading.

NATIONALITY
French

CURRENT CLUB
Los Angeles FC

DATE OF BIRTH	03/30/1986
POSITION	STRIKER
HEIGHT	6 FT. 4 IN.
PRO DEBUT	2005
PREFERRED FOOT	LEFT

GOALS
186

PENALTIES SCORED
21

APPEARANCES
489

ASSISTS
66

SHOT CONVERSION
16%

GOALS LEFT
112

MINUTES PER GOAL
167

GOALS RIGHT
16

HAT TRICKS
6

HEADED GOALS
57

SHOTS
1,173

MAJOR CLUB HONORS
⊕ Serie A: 2022 (AC Milan) ⚽ UEFA Champions League: 2021 (Chelsea) ⚽ UEFA Europa League: 2019 (Chelsea) ⊕ Ligue 1: 2012 (Montpellier) ⚽ FA Cup: 2014, 2015, 2017 (Arsenal), 2018 (Chelsea)

INTERNATIONAL HONORS
⊕ FIFA World Cup 2018, runner-up 2022
⊕ UEFA European Championship: Runner-up 2016

ACTIVITY AREAS

NATIONALITY
French

CURRENT CLUB
Atlético Madrid

ANTOINE GRIEZMANN

Known for being the ultimate team player, Antoine Griezmann is able to take on all offensive roles, be it front man, attacking midfielder, false number nine, or coming from wide positions. He is an excellent teammate, using his experience to improve everyone around him in all situations.

DATE OF BIRTH	03/21/1991
POSITION	STRIKER
HEIGHT	5 FT. 9¼ IN.
PRO DEBUT	2009
PREFERRED FOOT	LEFT

GOALS
226

PENALTIES SCORED
15

ASSISTS
91

APPEARANCES
587

SHOT CONVERSION
16%

MINUTES PER GOAL
201

GOALS LEFT
165

GOALS RIGHT
31

HAT TRICKS
5

HEADED GOALS
30

SHOTS
1,402

MAJOR CLUB HONORS
- UEFA Champions League: Runner-up 2016
- UEFA Europa League 2018 • UEFA Super Cup 2018
- Copa del Rey 2021 (Barcelona)

INTERNATIONAL HONORS
- FIFA World Cup: 2018, runner-up 2022
- UEFA European Championship: Runner-up 2016
- UEFA Nations League: 2021

ACTIVITY AREAS

ERLING HAALAND

Erling Haaland has become one of the most exciting forwards in world soccer. He has all the talents of a world class striker, including two good feet, blistering pace, good in the air, energy, strength, timing, and the instincts to put the ball in the back of the net.

NATIONALITY
Norwegian

CURRENT CLUB
Manchester City

DATE OF BIRTH	07/21/2000
POSITION	STRIKER
HEIGHT	6 FT. 4¼ IN.
PRO DEBUT	2015
PREFERRED FOOT	LEFT

GOALS
166

PENALTIES SCORED
28

APPEARANCES
172

ASSISTS
33

SHOT CONVERSION
28%

MINUTES PER GOAL
83

GOALS LEFT
120

GOALS RIGHT
25

HAT TRICKS
11

HEADED GOALS
20

SHOTS
594

MAJOR CLUB HONORS
⚽ Premier League: 2023, 2024 ⚽ UEFA Champions League: 2023 ⚽ DFB-Pokal: 2021 (Borussia Dortmund) ⚽ Austrian Bundesliga: 2019, 2020 (Red Bull Salzburg) ⚽ FA Cup: 2023, runner-up 2024 ⚽ Austrian Cup: 2019 (Red Bull Salzburg)

INTERNATIONAL HONORS
⚽ None to date

ACTIVITY AREAS

17

NATIONALITY
Italian

CURRENT CLUB
Besiktas

CIRO IMMOBILE

A great team player, Ciro Immobile is a natural finisher who is excellent in the air. His goals tally is even higher, because he refuses to give up lost causes and is willing to chase back to force mistakes out of defenders.

DATE OF BIRTH	02/20/1990
POSITION	STRIKER
HEIGHT	6 FT. ¾ IN.
PRO DEBUT	2007
PREFERRED FOOT	RIGHT

GOALS
220

PENALTIES SCORED
56

APPEARANCES
410

ASSISTS
51

SHOT CONVERSION
19%

MINUTES PER GOAL
135

GOALS LEFT
32

GOALS RIGHT
165

HAT TRICKS
7

HEADED GOALS
23

SHOTS
1,177

MAJOR CLUB HONORS
⚽ Serie A: Runner-up 2023 (Lazio)
⚽ Coppa Italia: 2019 (Lazio)

INTERNATIONAL HONORS
⚽ UEFA European Championship: 2020
⚽ UEFA Nations League: Third place 2023

ACTIVITY AREAS

DIOGO JOTA

Although most effective as a main striker, Diogo Jota is able to adapt his game to play deeper or as a left winger. In this role, he is master at waiting for defenders to be dragged out of position before running into spaces behind them and shooting powerfully with his right foot.

NATIONALITY
Portuguese

CURRENT CLUB
Liverpool

20

DATE OF BIRTH	12/04/1996
POSITION	STRIKER
HEIGHT	5 FT. 10 IN.
PRO DEBUT	2014
PREFERRED FOOT	RIGHT

GOALS
80

PENALTIES SCORED
1

ASSISTS
28

APPEARANCES
242

SHOT CONVERSION
16%

MINUTES PER GOAL
198

GOALS LEFT
30

GOALS RIGHT
40

HAT TRICKS
2

HEADED GOALS
10

SHOTS
516

MAJOR CLUB HONORS
⚽ UEFA Champions League: Runner-up 2022
⚽ FA Cup: 2022
⚽ EFL Cup: 2022

INTERNATIONAL HONORS
⚽ UEFA Nations League: 2019

ACTIVITY AREAS

15

NATIONALITY
Serbian

CURRENT CLUB
Fiorentina

LUKA JOVIĆ

Luka Jović is a predator in the penalty box. He uses his speed and attacking instincts to find spaces in the penalty area and score goals from close range with deft touches from either foot and occasionally his head.

DATE OF BIRTH	12/23/1997
POSITION	STRIKER
HEIGHT	6 FT. 10¼ IN.
PRO DEBUT	2014
PREFERRED FOOT	RIGHT

GOALS
50

PENALTIES SCORED
1

ASSISTS
14

APPEARANCES
187

SHOT CONVERSION
16%

MINUTES PER GOAL
167

GOALS LEFT
17

GOALS RIGHT
20

HAT TRICKS
1

HEADED GOALS
13

SHOTS
322

MAJOR CLUB HONORS
⚽ La Liga: 2020, 2022 (Real Madrid)
⚽ UEFA Champions League: 2022 (Real Madrid)
⚽ DFB-Pokal: 2018 (Eintracht Frankfurt)

INTERNATIONAL HONORS
⚽ None to date

ACTIVITY AREAS

HARRY KANE

Harry Kane has grown into the complete striker. His power in the air, skills with both feet, and superb ball-striking technique make him hard to defend against. What's more, with his defense-splitting passes, he also sets up many goals for his teammates.

NATIONALITY
English

CURRENT CLUB
Bayern Munich

DATE OF BIRTH	07/28/1993
POSITION	STRIKER
HEIGHT	6 FT. 2 IN.
PRO DEBUT	2009
PREFERRED FOOT	RIGHT

GOALS
282

PENALTIES SCORED
45

ASSISTS
64

APPEARANCES
400

SHOT CONVERSION
19%

GOALS RIGHT
172

GOALS LEFT
53

MINUTES PER GOAL
120

HAT TRICKS
14

HEADED GOALS
55

SHOTS
1,493

MAJOR CLUB HONORS
⚽ UEFA Champions League: Runner-up 2019 (Tottenham Hotspur)

INTERNATIONAL HONORS
⚽ UEFA European Championship: Runner-up 2020 (2021), runner-up 2024
⚽ UEFA Nations League: Third place 2019

ACTIVITY AREAS

NATIONALITY
Polish

CURRENT CLUB
Barcelona

ROBERT LEWANDOWSKI

Robert Lewandowski has consistently ranked as one of the world's best strikers since he made his debut at Borussia Dortmund in 2010. His positioning, technique, power, and finishing saw him net more than 300 goals in the Bundesliga before he made his move to Barcelona in 2022.

DATE OF BIRTH	08/21/1988
POSITION	STRIKER
HEIGHT	6 FT. ¾ IN.
PRO DEBUT	2005
PREFERRED FOOT	RIGHT

GOALS
448

PENALTIES SCORED
60

APPEARANCES
573

ASSISTS
90

SHOT CONVERSION
20%

MINUTES PER GOAL
105

GOALS LEFT
74

GOALS RIGHT
299

HAT TRICKS
23

HEADED GOALS
72

SHOTS
2,187

MAJOR CLUB HONORS
⚽ La Liga: 2023 ⚽ Bundesliga: 2011, 2012 (all B. Dortmund), 2015, '16, '17, '18, '19, '20, '21, '22 (all B. Munich) ⚽ UEFA Champions League: 2020 (B. Munich) ⚽ FIFA Club World Cup: 2020 (B. Munich) ⚽ UEFA Super Cup: 2020 (B. Munich)

INTERNATIONAL HONORS
⚽ None to date

ACTIVITY AREAS

ROMELU LUKAKU

Romelu Lukaku has a breathtaking pace and dribbling ability. Although he normally plays on the wing, he can also be dangerous in midfield, because he can leap high to win headers and shoot powerfully with either foot.

NATIONALITY
Belgian

CURRENT CLUB
AS Roma (on loan)

90

DATE OF BIRTH	05/13/1993
POSITION	STRIKER
HEIGHT	6 FT. 3 IN.
PRO DEBUT	2009
PREFERRED FOOT	LEFT

GOALS
209

PENALTIES SCORED
22

ASSISTS
61

APPEARANCES
448

SHOT CONVERSION
19%

MINUTES PER GOAL
160

GOALS LEFT
116

GOALS RIGHT
52

HAT TRICKS
3

HEADED GOALS
37

SHOTS
1,119

MAJOR CLUB HONORS
⚽ Serie A: 2021 (Int. Milan) ⚽ UEFA Champions League: Runner-up 2023 (Int. Milan) ⚽ Coppa Italia: 2023 (Int. Milan) ⚽ FIFA Club World Cup: 2021 (Chelsea) ⚽ UEFA Europa League: Runner-up 2020 (Chelsea) ⚽ Belgian Pro League: 2010 (Anderlecht)

INTERNATIONAL HONORS
⚽ FIFA World Cup: Third place 2018

ACTIVITY AREAS

NATIONALITY
French

CURRENT CLUB
Real Madrid

KYLIAN MBAPPÉ

A FIFA World Cup winner with France at just 18 and a runner-up four years later, Kylian Mbappé is counted among the best strikers in world soccer today. The fast-pace finisher is a superb ball player who consistently gets on the score sheet and sets up chances for his teammates.

DATE OF BIRTH	12/20/1998
POSITION	STRIKER
HEIGHT	5 FT. 10 IN.
PRO DEBUT	2015
PREFERRED FOOT	RIGHT

GOALS
239

PENALTIES SCORED
26

ASSISTS
88

APPEARANCES
319

SHOT CONVERSION
22%

MINUTES PER GOAL
101

GOALS LEFT
47

GOALS RIGHT
184

HAT TRICKS
11

HEADED GOALS
8

SHOTS
1,106

MAJOR CLUB HONORS
⚽ Ligue 1: 2017 (Monaco), 2018, 2019, 2020, 2022, 2023, 2024 ⚽ UEFA Champions League: Runner-up 2020
⚽ Coupe de France: 2018, 2020, 2021, 2024

INTERNATIONAL HONORS
⚽ FIFA World Cup: 2018, runner-up 2022
⚽ UEFA Nations League: 2021

ACTIVITY AREAS

LIONEL MESSI

The greatest player of his generation, if not the greatest ever, the 2022 World Cup winner is a fine playmaker with a stunning goal-scoring record. He is also a fantastically fast dribbler who can carve out opportunities to shoot with either foot, from any range, and rarely misses the target.

NATIONALITY
Argentinian

CURRENT CLUB
Inter Miami

10

DATE OF BIRTH	06/24/1987
POSITION	FORWARD
HEIGHT	5 FT. 6½ IN.
PRO DEBUT	2003
PREFERRED FOOT	LEFT

GOALS
637

PENALTIES SCORED
79

APPEARANCES
751

ASSISTS
272

SHOT CONVERSION
19%

MINUTES PER GOAL
97

GOALS LEFT
529

GOALS RIGHT
85

HAT TRICKS
44

HEADED GOALS
21

SHOTS
3,370

MAJOR CLUB HONORS
⚽ Ligue 1: 2022, 2023 (PSG) ⚽ La Liga: 2005, '06, '09, '10 '11, '13, '15, '16, '18, '19 (all Barça) ⚽ UEFA Champions League: 2006, '09, '11, '15 (all Barça) ⚽ UEFA Super Cup: 2009, '11, '15 (all Barça) ⚽ FIFA Club World Cup: 2009, '11, '15 (all Barça) ⚽ MLS Leagues Cup: 2023

INTERNATIONAL HONORS
⚽ FIFA World Cup: 2022, runner-up 2014
⚽ Olympic Games: Gold medal 2008
⚽ Copa América: 2021, 2024, runner-up* 2007*, 2015*, 2016*

ACTIVITY AREAS

75

7

NATIONALITY
Spanish

CURRENT CLUB
AC Milan

ÁLVARO MORATA

Álvaro Morata is perfectly built for a center striker. Tall, strong, and excellent in the air, he is comfortable with the ball at his feet. Morata is also surprisingly fast and has great tactical and positional awareness.

DATE OF BIRTH	10/23/1992
POSITION	STRIKER
HEIGHT	6 FT. 2½ IN.
PRO DEBUT	2010
PREFERRED FOOT	RIGHT

GOALS 150

PENALTIES SCORED 5

ASSISTS 55

APPEARANCES 439

SHOT CONVERSION 18%

MINUTES PER GOAL 161

GOALS LEFT 38

GOALS RIGHT 74

HAT TRICKS 3

HEADED GOALS 38

SHOTS 838

MAJOR CLUB HONORS

- ⚽ La Liga: 2012, 2017 (R. Madrid) ⚽ Serie A: 2015, 2016 (all Juventus)
- ⚽ UEFA Champions League: 2014, '17 (R. Madrid), runner-up 2015 (Juventus)
- ⚽ UEFA Europa League: 2019 (Chelsea) ⚽ UEFA Super Cup: 2016 (R. Madrid)
- ⚽ FIFA Club World Cup: 2016 (R. Madrid)

INTERNATIONAL HONORS

- ⚽ UEFA European Championship: 2024
- ⚽ UEFA Nations League: 2023
- ⚽ UEFA European U-21 Championship: 2013

ACTIVITY AREAS

NEYMAR

Counted among the long line of great Brazilian strikers to become a superstar, Neymar moved to the Saudi Pro League in 2023. His pace and phenomenal dribbling help him beat defenders in numbers. He strikes fear into the opposition defense with his energetic pace and playmaking skills.

NATIONALITY
Brazilian

CURRENT CLUB
Al Hilal

10

DATE OF BIRTH	02/05/1992
POSITION	FORWARD
HEIGHT	5 FT. 9 IN.
PRO DEBUT	2009
PREFERRED FOOT	RIGHT

GOALS
193

PENALTIES SCORED
34

ASSISTS
118

APPEARANCES
319

SHOT CONVERSION
19%

MINUTES PER GOAL
137

GOALS LEFT
52

GOALS RIGHT
134

HAT TRICKS
8

HEADED GOALS
7

SHOTS
1,038

MAJOR CLUB HONORS
⚽ La Liga: 2015, '16, '17 (all Barça) ⚽ Ligue 1: 2018, '19 '20, 2022, 2023 (all PSG) ⚽ UEFA Champions League: 2016 (Barça) ⚽ FIFA Club World Cup: 2016 (Barça) ⚽ Copa del Rey: 2015, '16, '17 (all Barça) ⚽ Coupe de France: 2018, '20, '21 (all PSG)

INTERNATIONAL HONORS
⚽ Copa América: Runner-up 2021
⚽ FIFA Confederations Cup: 2013
⚽ Olympic Games: Silver medal 2012, gold medal 2016

ACTIVITY AREAS

NATIONALITY
English

CURRENT CLUB
Manchester United

MARCUS RASHFORD

A great player to watch when he is on form, Marcus Rashford has scored some stunning goals for both club and country. He prefers to raid from the left side, to be on his stronger right foot, but his pace and heading ability make him just as dangerous in the middle.

DATE OF BIRTH	10/31/1997
POSITION	FORWARD
HEIGHT	5 FT. 10¾ in.
PRO DEBUT	2015
PREFERRED FOOT	RIGHT

GOALS
95

PENALTIES SCORED
10

APPEARANCES
305

ASSISTS
42

SHOT CONVERSION
15%

GOALS LEFT
12

MINUTES PER GOAL
218

GOALS RIGHT
75

HAT TRICKS
1

HEADED GOALS
8

SHOTS
653

MAJOR CLUB HONORS
⚽ UEFA Europa League: 2017, runner-up 2021
⚽ FA Cup: 2016, runner-up 2023, 2024
⚽ EFL Cup: 2023

INTERNATIONAL HONORS
⚽ UEFA European Championship: Runner-up 2021
⚽ UEFA Nations League: Third place 2019

ACTIVITY AREAS

MARCO REUS

Marco Reus is an attacker who can lead the frontline, play as a second striker, or play out wide. He is an expert finisher, especially with his right foot, and is also fantastic at setting up chances for his teammates. Reus parted ways with Dortmund in 2024 after serving the club for 12 seasons.

NATIONALITY
German

CURRENT CLUB
TBC

DATE OF BIRTH	05/31/1989
POSITION	FORWARD
HEIGHT	5 FT. 10¾ in.
PRO DEBUT	2006
PREFERRED FOOT	RIGHT

GOALS
180

PENALTIES SCORED
18

APPEARANCES
463

ASSISTS
108

SHOT CONVERSION
17%

MINUTES PER GOAL
195

GOALS LEFT
43

GOALS RIGHT
131

HAT TRICKS
3

HEADED GOALS
6

SHOTS
1,080

MAJOR CLUB HONORS
⚽ Bundesliga: runner-up 2023 (B. Dortmund) ⚽ UEFA Champions League: runner-up 2013 (B. Dortmund), runner-up 2024 (B. Dortmund) ⚽ DFB-Pokal: 2017, 2021, runner-up* 2014*, 2015*, 2016* (all B. Dortmund)

INTERNATIONAL HONORS
⚽ None to date

ACTIVITY AREAS

7

NATIONALITY
Portuguese

CURRENT CLUB
Al Nassr

CRISTIANO RONALDO

The superstar striker—now playing in Saudi Arabia—has wowed fans across the world with his all-around attacking skills. He is breathtaking to watch when he is running at defenses, great in the air, and a superb finisher with an extraordinary goal-scoring record.

DATE OF BIRTH	02/05/1985
POSITION	FORWARD
HEIGHT	6 FT. 2 IN.
PRO DEBUT	2002
PREFERRED FOOT	RIGHT

GOALS
675

PENALTIES SCORED
130

ASSISTS
184

APPEARANCES
782

SHOT CONVERSION
15%

MINUTES PER GOAL
98

GOALS LEFT
116

GOALS RIGHT
449

HAT TRICKS
53

HEADED GOALS
108

SHOTS
4,556

MAJOR CLUB HONORS

⚽ UEFA Champions League: 2008 (Man. U), 2014, '16, '17, '18 (R. Madrid) ⚽ FIFA Club World Cup: 2008 (Man. U), 2014, '16, '17 (R. Madrid) ⚽ UEFA Super Cup: 2014, '17 (R. Madrid) ⚽ Serie A: 2019, '20 (Juventus) ⚽ Premier League: 2007, '08, '09 (Man. U) ⚽ La Liga: 2012, '17 (R. Madrid)

INTERNATIONAL HONORS

⚽ UEFA European Championship: 2016
⚽ UEFA Nations League: 2019

ACTIVITY AREAS

MOHAMED SALAH

The two-time African Footballer [Soccer Player] Of The Year is a great left-footed attacker who prowls the left wing. Mo Salah has amazing pace with the ability to make angled runs, finding gaps in defenses before scoring spectacular goals.

NATIONALITY
Egyptian

CURRENT CLUB
Liverpool

DATE OF BIRTH	06/15/1992
POSITION	WINGER
HEIGHT	5 FT. 9 IN.
PRO DEBUT	2010
PREFERRED FOOT	LEFT

GOALS
236

PENALTIES SCORED
30

APPEARANCES
423

ASSISTS
102

SHOT CONVERSION
17%

MINUTES PER GOAL
143

GOALS LEFT
190

GOALS RIGHT
36

HAT TRICKS
6

HEADED GOALS
10

SHOTS
1,368

MAJOR CLUB HONORS
⚽ Premier League: 2020 ⚽ UEFA Champions League: 2019, runner-up 2018, runner-up 2022 ⚽ UEFA Super Cup: 2019 ⚽ FIFA Club World Cup: 2019 ⚽ FA Cup: 2022

INTERNATIONAL HONORS
⚽ CAF Africa Cup of Nations: Runner-up 2017, runner-up 2021

ACTIVITY AREAS

7

NATIONALITY
South Korean

CURRENT CLUB
Tottenham Hotspur

SON HEUNG-MIN

Son Heung-Min is at his best when he plays behind the main striker. Although excellent with both feet, attacking from the right side is his strength, and he converts a lot of chances that are set up by knockdowns or passes across the box.

DATE OF BIRTH	07/08/1992
POSITION	WINGER
HEIGHT	6 FT. ¼ IN.
PRO DEBUT	2010
PREFERRED FOOT	BOTH

GOALS
181

PENALTIES SCORED
3

ASSISTS
75

APPEARANCES
496

SHOT CONVERSION
17%

MINUTES PER GOAL
195

GOALS LEFT
70

GOALS RIGHT
102

HAT TRICKS
6

HEADED GOALS
9

SHOTS
1,091

MAJOR CLUB HONORS
⚽ UEFA Champions League: Runner-up 2019

INTERNATIONAL HONORS
⚽ AFC Asian Cup: Runner-up 2015

ACTIVITY AREAS

VINÍCIUS JÚNIOR

Vinícius Júnior loves terrorizing right backs, attacking off the left flank, cutting inside to deliver crosses or shooting with his favored right foot. He brings flair and panache, combined with blistering pace and fantastic dribbling, making him truly world class on his day.

NATIONALITY
Brazilian

CURRENT CLUB
Real Madrid

7

DATE OF BIRTH	07/12/2000
POSITION	WINGER
HEIGHT	5 FT. 9¼ IN.
PRO DEBUT	2017
PREFERRED FOOT	RIGHT

GOALS
71

PENALTIES SCORED
2

ASSISTS
47

APPEARANCES
232

SHOT CONVERSION
15%

MINUTES PER GOAL
222

GOALS LEFT
11

GOALS RIGHT
53

HAT TRICKS
1

HEADED GOALS
5

SHOTS
479

MAJOR CLUB HONORS
⚽ UEFA Champions League: 2022, 2024 ⚽ La Liga: 2020, 2022, 2024 ⚽ FIFA Club World Cup: 2018, 2022 ⚽ UEFA Super Cup: 2022 ⚽ Copa del Rey: 2023

INTERNATIONAL HONORS
⚽ -None to date

ACTIVITY AREAS

GOALKEEPERS

The goalkeeper is a team's last line of defense and, unlike the other positions, there is no one playing next to them. There is more pressure on goalkeepers than in any other position, because when a keeper makes an error, the chances are that the other team will score. The goalies featured in this section are all great shot stoppers, but some play outside their penalty areas as sweeper keepers; others have made their reputation as penalty savers; and then there are those who are great at catching the ball or punching it clear.

WHAT DO THE STATS MEAN?

CATCHES
This is the number of times the keeper has dealt with an attack—usually a cross—by catching the ball.

CLEAN SHEETS
Any occasion on which the goalie has not let in a goal for the full duration of the game counts as a clean sheet.

GOALS CONCEDED
This is the number of goals the keeper has conceded in his career in top-division soccer.

PENALTIES FACED/SAVED
This is the number of times a goalie has faced a penalty (excludes shootouts) and how successful he has been at saving it.

PUNCHES
This is a measure of how often the keeper has dealt with a dangerous ball (usually a cross) by punching it clear.

SAVES
This shows how many times the goalkeeper has stopped a shot or header that was on target.

Did you know?

Goalkeepers can, in theory, score goals with their hands. If they throw a ball downfield and it goes directly into the opposition net, the goal will count but, of course, the ball would have to travel more than 100 yards, which is unlikely.

1

NATIONALITY
Brazilian

CURRENT CLUB
Liverpool

ALISSON

The Brazilian has proved to be a top keeper at Liverpool. Alisson is a superb shot stopper and great at dealing with crosses. Incredibly quick off his line to foil any threat, he can turn defense into attack by finding teammates with long or short passes.

DATE OF BIRTH	10/02/1992
POSITION	GOALKEEPER
HEIGHT	6 FT. 4 IN.
PRO DEBUT	2013
PREFERRED FOOT	RIGHT

GOALS CONCEDED
281

APPEARANCES
308

PENALTIES SAVED
5

CLEAN SHEETS
132

SAVES
793

PENALTIES FACED
22

CATCHES
136

PUNCHES
119

MAJOR CLUB HONORS
- ⚽ Premier League: 2020
- ⚽ UEFA Champions League: 2019, runner-up 2022
- ⚽ FIFA Club World Cup: 2019
- ⚽ FA Cup: 2022

INTERNATIONAL HONORS
- ⚽ Copa América: 2019, runner-up 2021

ACTIVITY AREAS

CLAUDIO BRAVO

Claudio Bravo is an accomplished presence in goal with high levels of composure and concentration. As well as being comfortable with the ball at his feet and a good distributor, he is a great shot stopper, especially when facing penalty kicks. Bravo left Real Betis in 2024 after four seasons.

NATIONALITY
Chilean

CURRENT CLUB
TBC

DATE OF BIRTH	04/13/1983
POSITION	GOALKEEPER
HEIGHT	6 FT. ¼ IN.
PRO DEBUT	2002
PREFERRED FOOT	RIGHT

GOALS CONCEDED
407

APPEARANCES
351

PENALTIES SAVED
6

CLEAN SHEETS
117

SAVES
996

PENALTIES FACED
33

CATCHES
360

PUNCHES
159

MAJOR CLUB HONORS
⚽ UEFA Champions League: 2015 (Barcelona) ⚽ La Liga: 2015, 2016 (Barcelona) ⚽ Premier League: 2018 (Man. City) ⚽ FIFA Club World Cup: 2015 (Barcelona) ⚽ UEFA Super Cup: 2015 (Barcelona)

INTERNATIONAL HONORS
⚽ Copa América: 2015, 2016 ⚽ FIFA Confederations Cup: Runner-up 2017

ACTIVITY AREAS

NATIONALITY
Belgian

CURRENT CLUB
Real Madrid

THIBAUT COURTOIS

Thibaut Courtois uses his height to dominate his penalty area, catching crosses and punching well. An agile shot stopper, he can get down low to make saves, communicates well with his defense, is excellent coming off his line, and passes well.

DATE OF BIRTH	05/11/1992
POSITION	GOALKEEPER
HEIGHT	6 FT. 6¼ IN.
PRO DEBUT	2009
PREFERRED FOOT	LEFT

GOALS CONCEDED
454

APPEARANCES
497

PENALTIES SAVED
8

SAVES
1,257

CLEAN SHEETS
211

PENALTIES FACED
44

CATCHES
505

PUNCHES
144

MAJOR CLUB HONORS
⚽ La Liga: 2014 (Atlético. Madrid), 2020, 2022, runner-up 2023, 2024 ⚽ Prem. League: 2015, 2017 (all Chelsea) ⚽ UEFA Champions League: 2022, 2024 ⚽ UEFA Europa League: 2012 (Atlético Madrid) ⚽ FIFA Club World Cup: 2018 ⚽ UEFA Super Cup: 2012 (Atlético Madrid) 2022

INTERNATIONAL HONORS
⚽ FIFA World Cup: Third place 2018

ACTIVITY AREAS

GIANLUIGI DONNARUMMA

The Italian is an amazing talent who made his Serie A debut at the age of only 16, won his first Italian cap at 17, and became a European champion at 22. Mentally strong and composed under pressure, he has everything it takes to be an all-time great.

NATIONALITY
Italian

CURRENT CLUB
Paris Saint-Germain

DATE OF BIRTH	02/25/1999
POSITION	GOALKEEPER
HEIGHT	6 FT. 5 IN.
PRO DEBUT	2015
PREFERRED FOOT	RIGHT

GOALS CONCEDED
356

APPEARANCES
336

PENALTIES SAVED
11

CLEAN SHEETS
107

SAVES
998

PENALTIES FACED
49

CATCHES
207

PUNCHES
154

MAJOR CLUB HONORS
- Ligue 1: 2022, 2023, 2024
- Coupe de France: 2024
- Supercoppa Italiana: 2016 (AC Milan)

INTERNATIONAL HONORS
- UEFA European Championship: 2020 (2021)
- UEFA Nations League: Third place 2021, third place 2023

ACTIVITY AREAS

31

NATIONALITY
Brazilian

CURRENT CLUB
Manchester City

EDERSON

Due to his range of passing and great ball skills, Ederson is often considered a playmaker goalkeeper and counted as one of the best in the English Premier League. He is a fine shot stopper with a reputation for being a great penalty-kick saver, too.

DATE OF BIRTH	08/17/1993
POSITION	GOALKEEPER
HEIGHT	6 FT. 2 IN.
PRO DEBUT	2011
PREFERRED FOOT	LEFT

GOALS CONCEDED
266

APPEARANCES
330

PENALTIES SAVED
6

CLEAN SHEETS
142

SAVES
593

PENALTIES FACED
37

CATCHES
147

PUNCHES
80

MAJOR CLUB HONORS
⚽ Premier League: 2018, 2019, 2021, 2022, 2023, 2024
⚽ UEFA Champions League: Runner-up 2021, 2023
⚽ FA Cup: 2019, 2023, runner-up 2024

INTERNATIONAL HONORS
⚽ Copa América: 2019, runner-up 2021

ACTIVITY AREAS

PÉTER GULÁCSI

Péter Gulácsi is dedicated to preparing for every soccer situation he faces. He studies approaching forwards to get an instinct for where they will shoot, gets into the right position, and then makes difficult saves look easy.

NATIONALITY
Hungarian

CURRENT CLUB
RB Leipzig

DATE OF BIRTH	05/06/1990
POSITION	GOALKEEPER
HEIGHT	6 FT. 3 IN.
PRO DEBUT	2008
PREFERRED FOOT	RIGHT

GOALS CONCEDED
348

APPEARANCES
295

PENALTIES SAVED
3

CLEAN SHEETS
87

SAVES
711

PENALTIES FACED
36

CATCHES
187

PUNCHES
76

MAJOR CLUB HONORS
- ⚽ Austrian Bundesliga: 2014, 2015 (Red Bull Salzburg)
- ⚽ Austrian Cup: 2014, 2015 (Red Bull Salzburg)
- ⚽ DFB-Pokal: Runner-up* 2019*, 2021*, 2022, 2023

INTERNATIONAL HONORS
- ⚽ FIFA U-20 World Cup: Third place 2009

ACTIVITY AREAS

1

NATIONALITY
Finnish

CURRENT CLUB
Bayer Leverkusen

LUKAS HRADECKY

Like many goalkeepers, it wasn't until his thirties that Lukas Hradecky reached his peak. He is an excellent shot stopper with plenty of confidence, decisive when dealing with crosses, and great at organizing his penalty area and communicating with defenders.

DATE OF BIRTH	11/24/1989
POSITION	GOALKEEPER
HEIGHT	6 FT. 3½ IN.
PRO DEBUT	2008
PREFERRED FOOT	RIGHT

GOALS CONCEDED
426

APPEARANCES
337

PENALTIES SAVED
6

CLEAN SHEETS
95

SAVES
933

CATCHES
234

PENALTIES FACED
38

PUNCHES
124

MAJOR CLUB HONORS
⚽ Bundesliga: 2024
⚽ DFB Pokal: 2018 (Eintracht Frankfurt), 2024
⚽ UEFA Europa League: Runner-up 2024

INTERNATIONAL HONORS
⚽ Baltic Cup: Runner-up 2012

ACTIVITY AREAS

EMILIANO MARTÍNEZ

NATIONALITY
Argentinian

CURRENT CLUB
Aston Villa

An immensely athletic goalkeeper, Emiliano Martínez is capable of reaching shots going into the top corner with either hand. His quick feet mean he gets into good positions not only to make saves but also reduce the angle for shots.

DATE OF BIRTH	09/02/1992
POSITION	GOALKEEPER
HEIGHT	6 FT. 4¾ IN.
PRO DEBUT	2012
PREFERRED FOOT	RIGHT

GOALS CONCEDED
285

APPEARANCES
232

PENALTIES SAVED
6

CLEAN SHEETS
73

SAVES
711

PENALTIES FACED
29

CATCHES
286

PUNCHES
36

MAJOR CLUB HONORS
⚽ FA Cup: 2020 (Arsenal)

INTERNATIONAL HONORS
⚽ Copa América: 2021, 2024
⚽ FIFA World Cup: 2022

ACTIVITY AREAS

NATIONALITY
Costa Rican

CURRENT CLUB
TBC

KEYLOR NAVAS

Keylor Navas is strong, athletic, agile, a fine organizer, and shot stopper. Among the new breed of hyperaggressive keepers, he has the confidence to play off his lines, even in situations that might call for more restrained positioning. Navas left French club PSG in 2024 after five years.

DATE OF BIRTH	12/15/1986
POSITION	GOALKEEPER
HEIGHT	6 FT. ¾ IN.
PRO DEBUT	2005
PREFERRED FOOT	RIGHT

GOALS CONCEDED
310

APPEARANCES
316

PENALTIES SAVED
10

CLEAN SHEETS
113

SAVES
954

PENALTIES FACED
43

CATCHES
164

PUNCHES
135

MAJOR CLUB HONORS

⚽ Ligue 1: 2020, '22, '24 (all PSG) ⚽ La Liga: 2017 (R. Madrid) ⚽ UEFA Champions League: 2016, '17, '18 (all R. Madrid) runner-up 2020 (PSG) ⚽ FIFA World Club Cup: 2014, '16, '17, '18 (all R. Madrid) ⚽ UEFA Super Cup: 2017 (R. Madrid) ⚽ Coupe de France: 2024 (PSG)

INTERNATIONAL HONORS

⚽ None to date

ACTIVITY AREAS

MANUEL NEUER

Manuel Neuer is famous for being soccer's first sweeper keeper. He is a fine shot stopper who commands his penalty area and marshals the defense well. He is also great with the ball at his feet, allowing for defenders to play farther upfield.

NATIONALITY
German

CURRENT CLUB
Bayern Munich

DATE OF BIRTH	03/27/1986
POSITION	GOALKEEPER
HEIGHT	6 FT. 4 IN.
PRO DEBUT	2004
PREFERRED FOOT	RIGHT

GOALS CONCEDED
554

APPEARANCES
641

PENALTIES SAVED
12

SAVES
1,591

CLEAN SHEETS
280

PENALTIES FACED
48

PUNCHES
276

CATCHES
603

MAJOR CLUB HONORS
⚽ Bundesliga: 2013, '14, '15, '16, '17, '18, '19, '20, '21, '22, '23 ⚽ UEFA Champions League: 2013, 2020 ⚽ UEFA Super Cup: 2013, 2020 ⚽ FIFA Club World Cup: 2013, 2020 ⚽ DFB Pokal: 2011 (Schalke 04) 2013' '14, '16, '19, '20

INTERNATIONAL HONORS
⚽ FIFA World Cup: 2014

ACTIVITY AREAS

13

NATIONALITY
Slovenian

CURRENT CLUB
Atlético Madrid

JAN OBLAK

One of the world's most accomplished keepers, Jan Oblak is blessed with quick reflexes and agility, and he's excellent at coming off his line and organizing his defense. His communication skills make him a reliable team vice captain.

DATE OF BIRTH	01/07/1993
POSITION	GOALKEEPER
HEIGHT	6 FT. 2 IN.
PRO DEBUT	2009
PREFERRED FOOT	RIGHT

GOALS CONCEDED
339

APPEARANCES
427

PENALTIES SAVED
9

SAVES
1,078

CLEAN SHEETS
199

PENALTIES FACED
43

CATCHES
261

PUNCHES
121

MAJOR CLUB HONORS
- ⚽ La Liga: 2021
- ⚽ UEFA Champions League: Runner-up 2016
- ⚽ UEFA Europa League: 2018
- ⚽ UEFA Super Cup: 2018

INTERNATIONAL HONORS
- ⚽ None to date

ACTIVITY AREAS

RUI PATRÍCIO

Rui Patrício is an old-fashioned continental goalkeeper, primarily a shot stopper who lets his defenders deal with crosses into the danger area. He has great instincts and anticipation and is expert at coming off his line to narrow angles.

NATIONALITY
Portuguese

CURRENT CLUB
TBC

DATE OF BIRTH	02/15/1988
POSITION	GOALKEEPER
HEIGHT	6 FT. 2½ IN.
PRO DEBUT	2006
PREFERRED FOOT	LEFT

GOALS CONCEDED 374

APPEARANCES 315

PENALTIES SAVED 6

SAVES 802

CLEAN SHEETS 98

PENALTIES FACED 36

PUNCHES 60

CATCHES 170

MAJOR CLUB HONORS
⚽ Europa Conference League: 2022 (Roma) ⚽ Taça de Portugal: 2007, 2008, 2015 (Sporting Clube)

INTERNATIONAL HONORS
⚽ UEFA European Championship: 2016
⚽ UEFA Nations League: 2019

ACTIVITY AREAS

NATIONALITY
English

CURRENT CLUB
Everton

JORDAN PICKFORD

Playing for a struggling team in Everton, Jordan Pickford is kept busy and is an excellent shot stopper. Not the tallest of goalkeepers, he prefers to punch instead of catch the ball and is also good at distributing to teammates.

DATE OF BIRTH	03/07/1994
POSITION	GOALKEEPER
HEIGHT	6 FT. ¾ IN.
PRO DEBUT	2011
PREFERRED FOOT	LEFT

GOALS CONCEDED
428

APPEARANCES
289

PENALTIES SAVED
5

CLEAN SHEETS
75

SAVES
918

PENALTIES FACED
37

CATCHES
176

PUNCHES
148

MAJOR CLUB HONORS
⚽ None to date

INTERNATIONAL HONORS
⚽ UEFA European Championship: Runner-up 2020, runner-up 2024
⚽ UEFA Natiom League: Third place 2019

ACTIVITY AREAS

NICK POPE

Since joining The Magpies, Nick Pope has proved his worth by keeping many clean sheets for his new club. He dominates his penalty area and is excellent at stopping shots, dealing with crosses, and being a sweeper keeper outside the box.

NATIONALITY
English

CURRENT CLUB
Newcastle United

22

DATE OF BIRTH	04/19/1992
POSITION	GOALKEEPER
HEIGHT	6 FT. 3 IN.
PRO DEBUT	2011
PREFERRED FOOT	RIGHT

GOALS CONCEDED
222

APPEARANCES
198

PENALTIES SAVED
4

SAVES
624

CLEAN SHEETS
66

PENALTIES FACED
24

PUNCHES
89

CATCHES
218

MAJOR CLUB HONORS
⚽ None to date

INTERNATIONAL HONORS
⚽ None to date

ACTIVITY AREAS

30

NATIONALITY
French

CURRENT CLUB
Lens

BRICE SAMBA

Brice Samba has the personality and physique to dominate his penalty area. His attributes include stopping shots from both long and close range, dealing with crosses, and starting attacks with kicks downfield. He is not afraid to make unorthodox saves either.

DATE OF BIRTH	04/25/1994
POSITION	GOALKEEPER
HEIGHT	6 FT. 1½ IN.
PRO DEBUT	2011
PREFERRED FOOT	LEFT

GOALS CONCEDED
135

APPEARANCES
121

PENALTIES SAVED
3

CLEAN SHEETS
41

SAVES
393

PENALTIES FACED
22

CATCHES
105

PUNCHES
19

MAJOR CLUB HONORS
⚽ None to date

INTERNATIONAL HONORS
⚽ None to date

ACTIVITY AREAS

100

YANN SOMMER

Yann Sommer is not tall for a goalkeeper but he has great anticipation, reflexes, and footwork that more than make up for his lack of height. A good shot stopper, he is comfortable playing as a sweeper keeper, too.

NATIONALITY
Swiss

CURRENT CLUB
Inter Milan

DATE OF BIRTH	12/17/1988
POSITION	GOALKEEPER
HEIGHT	6 FT.
PRO DEBUT	2005
PREFERRED FOOT	LEFT

GOALS CONCEDED **529**

APPEARANCES **408**

PENALTIES SAVED **6**

CLEAN SHEETS **120**

SAVES **1,330**

PENALTIES FACED **61**

CATCHES **393**

PUNCHES **130**

MAJOR CLUB HONORS
⚽ Serie A: 2024 ⚽ Bundesliga: 2023 (Bayern Munich)
⚽ Supercoppa Italiana: 2023

INTERNATIONAL HONORS
⚽ None to date

ACTIVITY AREAS

1

NATIONALITY
Polish

CURRENT CLUB
Juventus

WOJCIECH SZCZĘSNY

Wojciech Szczęsny has grown into one of Europe's top-class keepers. A natural shot stopper with lightning reflexes, he is also great at controlling his penalty area, dealing with crosses, and setting up counterattacks with quick clearances.

DATE OF BIRTH	04/18/1990
POSITION	GOALKEEPER
HEIGHT	6 FT. 4¾ IN.
PRO DEBUT	2009
PREFERRED FOOT	RIGHT

GOALS CONCEDED
497

APPEARANCES
480

PENALTIES SAVED
16

CLEAN SHEETS
173

SAVES
1,258

PENALTIES FACED
77

CATCHES
391

PUNCHES
190

MAJOR CLUB HONORS
⚽ Serie A: 2018, 2019, 2020 ⚽ FA Cup: 2014, 2015 (all Arsenal) ⚽ Coppa Italia: 2018, 2021, 2024 ⚽ Supercoppa Italiana: 2018, 2020

INTERNATIONAL HONORS
⚽ None to date

ACTIVITY AREAS

MARC-ANDRÉ TER STEGEN

A great sweeper keeper, Marc-André ter Stegen is simply world class. In addition to his fine goalkeeping qualities, he is exceptional at anticipating opponents who have beaten the offside trap and can rush off his line to meet the danger.

NATIONALITY
German

CURRENT CLUB
Barcelona

DATE OF BIRTH	04/30/1992
POSITION	GOALKEEPER
HEIGHT	6 FT. 1½ IN.
PRO DEBUT	2009
PREFERRED FOOT	RIGHT

GOALS CONCEDED
484

APPEARANCES
490

PENALTIES SAVED
7

CLEAN SHEETS
199

SAVES
1,360

PENALTIES FACED
49

CATCHES
473

PUNCHES
203

MAJOR CLUB HONORS

⚽ La Liga: 2015, 2016, 2018, 2019, 2023 ⚽ UEFA Champions League: 2015 ⚽ UEFA Super Cup: 2015 ⚽ FIFA Club World Cup: 2015 ⚽ Copa del Rey: 2015, 2016, 2017, 2018, 2021

INTERNATIONAL HONORS

⚽ FIFA Confederations Cup: 2017

ACTIVITY AREAS

MANAGERS

Head coaches are as different to each other as players who play in different positions. But the majority of the 12 featured in this section have one thing in common: they are all winners, either in their domestic leagues or in continental competitions. Some, such as Mikel Arteta (opposite), were successful players themselves and trophy winners well before they entered management, while others, such as Claudio Ranieri, had less fruitful playing careers but have enjoyed great success as the brains behind a top side.

WHAT DO THE STATS MEAN?

GAMES MANAGED
This is the number of matches the coach has been in charge of across his entire career in soccer management.

TEAMS MANAGED
The number of clubs (first teams only) that the coach has managed during his career to date.

WINS
This is the number of games the coach has won, including one leg of a cup tie, even if the tie was lost on aggregate or penalties.

TROPHIES
The trophy list features the head coach's success in domestic top divisions, national and league cups, and international club competitions, except any super cups.

Did you know?

Arsenal manager Mikel Arteta focuses on the relationship between himself and his players to bring the best out of his team. His willingness to listen to players while instilling high expectations helps forge team unity.

XABI ALONSO

Xabi Alonso is currently Europe's most in-demand coach after winning the Bundesliga title in his first full season. His teams play 3–4–2–1 formation, inviting pressure, then counterattacking and taking advantage of holes in the opposition's defenses.

NATIONALITY
Spanish

CURRENT CLUB
Bayer Leverkusen

YEARS AS HEAD COACH:	5

FIRST CLUB:	REAL SOCIEDAD B

CLUBS MANAGED	GAMES	LEAGUE TITLES
2	187	1

WINS	DRAW	LOSSES
99	42	46

CHAMPIONS LEAGUE TROPHIES	EUROPA LEAGUE TROPHIES	OTHER TROPHIES*
0	0	1

*Excludes Super Cups

MAJOR CLUB HONORS
- Bundesliga: 2024
- DFB-Pokal: 2024
- UEFA Europa League: Runner-up 2024

CARLO ANCELOTTI

The vastly experienced and accomplished Carlo Ancelotti uses different systems, depending on the opposition and players available. His favorite formation is 4–4–2, sometimes in a diamond, other times with four midfielders in a line across the field.

 NATIONALITY
Italian

CURRENT CLUB
Real Madrid

YEARS AS HEAD COACH :	29

FIRST CLUB:	REGGIANA

CLUBS MANAGED	GAMES	LEAGUE TITLES
10	1,339	6

WINS	DRAW	LOSSES
797	299	243

CHAMPIONS LEAGUE TROPHIES	EUROPA LEAGUE TROPHIES	OTHER TROPHIES*
5	0	10

*Excludes Super Cups

MAJOR CLUB HONORS
- La Liga: 2022, runner-up 2023, 2024
- UEFA Champions League: 2003, 2007 (all AC Milan), 2014, 2022, 2024
- FIFA Club World Cup: 2007 (AC Milan), 2014, 2022
- Serie A: 2004 (AC Milan)
- Premier League: 2010 (Chelsea)
- Ligue 1: 2013 (Paris St Germain)
- Copa del Rey: 2014, 2023
- Bundesliga: 2017 (Bayern Munich)

MIKEL ARTETA

Mikel Arteta gambled on taking a high-profile club as his first job in management. He changed his style from a defensively strong 5—4—1 to a more aggressive attacking 4—2—3—1, with players causing danger from anywhere on the field.

NATIONALITY
Spanish

CURRENT CLUB
Arsenal

YEARS AS HEAD COACH: 05

FIRST CLUB: ARSENAL

CLUBS MANAGED	GAMES	LEAGUE TITLES
1	232	0
WINS	**DRAW**	**LOSSES**
137	38	57
CHAMPIONS LEAGUE TROPHIES	**EUROPA LEAGUE TROPHIES**	**OTHER TROPHIES***
0	0	3

MAJOR CLUB HONORS
- ⚽ Premier League: Runner-up 2023, runner-up 2024
- ⚽ FA Cup: 2020
- ⚽ FA Community Shield: 2020, 2023

*Excludes Super Cups

UNAI EMERY

Unai Emery has enjoyed great success managing clubs that have a modest budget. His preference is either a 4—2—3—1 formation or 4—4—2, the choice depending on the attacking skills of the two center midfielders and their ability to retain possession.

NATIONALITY
Spanish

CURRENT CLUB
Aston Villa

YEARS AS HEAD COACH: 20

FIRST CLUB: LORCA DEPORTIVA

CLUBS MANAGED	GAMES	LEAGUE TITLES
9	1,009	1
WINS	**DRAW**	**LOSSES**
537	221	251
CHAMPIONS LEAGUE TROPHIES	**EUROPA LEAGUE TROPHIES**	**OTHER TROPHIES***
0	4	6

MAJOR CLUB HONORS
- ⚽ UEFA Europa League: 2014, 2015, 2016 (all Sevilla), 2021 (Villareal), runner-up 2019 (Arsenal)
- ⚽ Ligue 1: 2018 (Paris Saint-Germain)
- ⚽ Coupe de France: 2017, 2018 (all Paris Saint-Germain)

*Excludes Super Cups

LUIS ENRIQUE

Luis Enrique will not compromise his soccer beliefs, and he will play in the formation that suits his available players, normally 4—3—3 or 3—4—3. He wants his players to express themselves on the ball whenever possible.

NATIONALITY
Spanish

CURRENT CLUB
Paris Saint-Germain

YEARS AS HEAD COACH:	16

FIRST CLUB:	BARCELONA B

CLUBS MANAGED	GAMES	LEAGUE TITLES
5	440	3

WINS	DRAW	LOSSES
263	90	87

CHAMPIONS LEAGUE TROPHIES	EUROPA LEAGUE TROPHIES	OTHER TROPHIES*
1	0	6

*Excludes Super Cups

MAJOR CLUB HONORS
- UEFA Champions League; 2015 (Barcelona)
- Ligue 1: 2024
- La Liga; 2015, 2016 (Barcelona)
- FIFA World Club Cup; 2015 (Barcelona)
- Coupe de France: 2024
- Trophée des Champions: 2023
- Copa del Rey; 2015, 2016, 2017 (Barcelona)

GIAN PIERO GASPERINI

Gian Piero Gasperini wants his teams to be attacking, but to defend man-for-man when not in possession. His 3—4—3 formation is fluid; when his teams attack, the wing-backs play as wide midfielders and try to outnumber opposing defenders.

NATIONALITY
Italian

CURRENT CLUB
Atalanta

YEARS AS HEAD COACH:	22

FIRST CLUB:	CROTONE

CLUBS MANAGED	GAMES	LEAGUE TITLES
5	822	0

WINS	DRAW	LOSSES
375	198	249

CHAMPIONS LEAGUE TROPHIES	EUROPA LEAGUE TROPHIES	OTHER TROPHIES*
0	1	0

MAJOR CLUB HONORS
- UEFA Europa League: 2024

*Excludes Super Cups

PEP GUARDIOLA

Once a great midfielder himself, Pep Guardiola devised the *tika-taka* passing system at Barcelona (2008—12). Disciplined in possession, without the ball his teams press the opposition into making mistakes and then launch rapid counter-attacks.

NATIONALITY
Spanish

CURRENT CLUB
Manchester City

YEARS AS HEAD COACH: 17

FIRST CLUB: BARCELONA B

CLUBS MANAGED	GAMES	LEAGUE TITLES
4	922	12

WINS	DRAW	LOSSES
671	143	108

CHAMPIONS LEAGUE TROPHIES	EUROPA LEAGUE TROPHIES	OTHER TROPHIES*
3	0	15

*Excludes Super Cups

MAJOR CLUB HONORS
- ⚽ Premier League: 2018, 2019, 2021, 2022, 2023, 2024
- ⚽ UEFA Champions League: 2009, 2011 Barcelona), runner-up 2021, 2023
- ⚽ FIFA Club World Cup: 2009, 2011 (Barcelona), 2013 (B. Munich)
- ⚽ La Liga: 2009, 2010, 2011 (Barcelona)
- ⚽ Bundesliga: 2014, 2015, 2016 (B. Munich)
- ⚽ FA Cup: 2019, 2023, runner-up 2024

SIMONE INZAGHI

Simone Inzaghi's teams almost always play in a 3—5—2 formation. He likes his team to keep possession with short passes, patiently waiting to strike, and encourages his central defenders to draw opponents out of position to join attacks.

NATIONALITY
Italian

CURRENT CLUB
Inter Milan

YEARS AS HEAD COACH: 9

FIRST CLUB: LAZIO

CLUBS MANAGED	GAMES	LEAGUE TITLES
2	409	1

WINS	DRAW	LOSSES
238	73	98

CHAMPIONS LEAGUE TROPHIES	EUROPA LEAGUE TROPHIES	OTHER TROPHIES*
0	0	8

*Excludes Super Cups

MAJOR CLUB HONORS
- ⚽ Serie A: 2024
- ⚽ UEFA Champions League: Runner-up 2023
- ⚽ Coppa Italia: 2019 (Lazio), 2022, 2023

STEFANO PIOLI

Stefano Pioli is superb at instilling confidence into his players. This is partly because he is flexible with his tactics and focuses on the management of the individuals, getting the best out of them on the field. He favors a 4–2–3–1 formation.

NATIONALITY
Italian

CURRENT CLUB
AC Milan

YEARS AS HEAD COACH: 21

FIRST CLUB: SALERNITANA

CLUBS MANAGED	GAMES	LEAGUE TITLES
13	871	1

WINS	DRAW	LOSSES
364	250	257

CHAMPIONS LEAGUE TROPHIES	EUROPA LEAGUE TROPHIES	OTHER TROPHIES*
0	0	0

MAJOR CLUB HONORS
- ⚽ Serie A: 2022, runner-up 2024

*Excludes Super Cups

ANGE POSTECOGLU

Ange Postecoglou is not afraid to test himself in new environments, having coached in five different countries on three continents. A fan of a 4–2–3–1 formation, his teams play open attacking soccer in a style popular with supporters.

NATIONALITY
Australian

CURRENT CLUB
Tottenham Hotspur

YEARS AS HEAD COACH: 23

FIRST CLUB: SOUTH MELBOURNE

CLUBS MANAGED	GAMES	LEAGUE TITLES
8	585	7

WINS	DRAW	LOSSES
322	110	153

CHAMPIONS LEAGUE TROPHIES	EUROPA LEAGUE TROPHIES	OTHER TROPHIES*
0	0	6

MAJOR CLUB HONORS
- ⚽ National Soccer League Champions: 1998, 1999 (South Melbourne)
- ⚽ OFC Club Championship: 1999 (South Melbourne)
- ⚽ A-League: 2011, 2012 (Brisbane Road)
- ⚽ J1 League: 2019 (Yokohama F Marinos)
- ⚽ Scottish Premiership: 2022, 2023 (Celtic)
- ⚽ Scottish Cup: 2023 (Celtic)

*Excludes Super Cups

DIEGO SIMEONE

Diego Simeone likes to use a formation that is almost a 4–2–2–2 unit, with wide midfielders playing between the two center ones and the strikers. Strong defensively, his teams are great at defending set pieces and dangerous in attack.

NATIONALITY
Argentinian

CURRENT CLUB
Atlético Madrid

YEARS AS HEAD COACH: 17

FIRST CLUB: RACING CLUB

CLUBS MANAGED	GAMES	LEAGUE TITLES
7	886	4

WINS	DRAW	LOSSES
497	204	185

CHAMPIONS LEAGUE TROPHIES	EUROPA LEAGUE TROPHIES	OTHER TROPHIES*
0	2	2

MAJOR CLUB HONORS
- ⚽ UEFA Champions League: Runner-up 2014, 2016
- ⚽ UEFA Europa League: 2012, 2018
- ⚽ UEFA Super Cup: 2012, 2018
- ⚽ La Liga: 2014, 2021
- ⚽ Copa del Rey: 2013
- ⚽ Primera División Apertura 2006 (Estudiantes)
- ⚽ Primera División Clausura 2008 (Racing Club)

*Excludes Super Cups

ARNE SLOT

Arne Slot is an astute and innovative coach. He has a reputation for developing young players and playing attractive, attacking football in a 4–3–3 formation. He sometimes operates a 4–2–3–1 line up, with two midfielders in front of the back four.

NATIONALITY
Dutch

CURRENT CLUB
Liverpool

YEARS AS HEAD COACH: 8

FIRST CLUB: SC CAMBUUR

CLUBS MANAGED	GAMES	LEAGUE TITLES
3	242	1

WINS	DRAW	LOSSES
151	51	40

CHAMPIONS LEAGUE TROPHIES	EUROPA LEAGUE TROPHIES	OTHER TROPHIES*
0	0	1

MAJOR CLUB HONORS
- ⚽ Eredivisie: 2023 (Feyenoord)
- ⚽ KNVB Cup: 2024 (Feyenoord)
- ⚽ UEFA Europa Conference 2022 (Feyenoord)

*Excludes Super Cups

NOTES